The Parent Playbooks

2nd Edition
Fun and Enjoyable Learning Activities with Kids

GRADES K - 2

Standards-Based Learning Activities

- Parent-Teacher tested
- Parent-Teacher contributed
- Fun ways to learn new ideas and apply old ones

Dr. Joni Samples

The Parent Playbooks: Grades K - 2

© 2019 ENGAGE! Press
Printed and bound in the United States of America

All rights reserved. Written permission must be secured from the publisher and author to use or reproduce any part of this book except for brief quotations in critical reviews or articles. To order additional copies, please contact the Publisher, Engage! Press at:

> ENGAGE! Press
> 2485 Notre Dame Blvd 370-170
> Chico, CA 95928
> www.engagepress.com

This book contains information gathered from many sources. The printer, publisher, and author disclaim any personal liability, either directly or indirectly, for advice or information presented within. Although the author, publisher, and printer have used care and diligence in the presentation, and made every effort to ensure the accuracy and completeness of the information contained in this book, we assume no responsibility for errors, inaccuracies, omissions, or any inconsistency herein.

First Printing 2019
ISBN No. 978-0-9906335-2-5
Library of Congress Cataloging–in–Publication Data

DEDICATION

The Parent Playbook series is dedicated to the memory of Linda Armstrong. Linda was a lover of books and literature, a librarian and writer, my editor and keeper of databases, believer in families and learning, and, above all, my friend.

ABOUT YOUR PARENT PLAYBOOK

Dear Parents,

Welcome to the Parent Playbook series, where you will find recipes for learning. Similar to a cookbook, each activity begins with a list of needed materials, the time required to complete the activity, and a description of the activity. Instead of a "daily nutritional requirement," these recipes relate to State Educational Standards for learning. The activities are easy and fun.

I am a lifelong educator with four children. During my child rearing days, my cooking rarely came from a cookbook. Meal planning consisted of whatever I could recall from my childhood or what would heat up quickly in the microwave.

My interest in assisting my children in education focused on, like my menu for meals, something quick, easy, and able to make a positive difference in a fun way. However, there was nothing available on the market that gave me easy directions and ideas to help my children become successful learners. I dredged stuff up from my teaching days or depended on their schools to provide something. But, homework didn't entertain me or my children enough to do more than what was due the next day. We would lose interest, so I began creating other activities to do.

It was then that my husband suggested that I write a column in the newspaper to share the activities with other parents. As the newly elected County Superintendent of Schools in our area and someone who wanted to let folks know I was on the job, that sounded like a winning idea. I could provide teachers, parents, and myself with home activities that were easy, fun and enhanced learning.

One day a colleague remarked, "That muffin activity sure did a lot of measuring of fractions. Which grade level standard is that?" Of course! Share activities and match them to the learning standards taught in the classroom and everyone wins. With that the idea for the Parent Playbooks was born.

Parents enjoy a fun learning time with their children. The activities they do together reinforce concepts taught at school. The teachers see the support from home reflected in the children's schoolwork. In addition, the kids—their grades, test scores and self-confidence are off the charts. So, here you have recipes for learning in the form of Parent Playbooks.

Taste, benefit from, and most of all experience the delicious joy of learning with your children.

Sincerely,
Dr. Joni

A Letter from Dr. Joni and Trinidad:

To the Kids

Trinidad says hi and welcome to The Parent Playbooks — a place where learning is fun!

You might think Trinidad learns mostly at the beach, but this is one starfish that gets around town. Grocery stores, movies, pizza parlors, and the library are just a few of the spots Trinidad is likely to show up. See how often you can find Trinidad as you and your family learn through the activities shared in this book. Don't forget to create your own activities. There is plenty of room for you and your family to write in the "What We Learned Today" section.

Enjoy the activities along with Trinidad and Make Learning Fun!

Sincerely,

Dr. Joni and Trinidad

Table of Contents

About the Learning Standards — 1

English Language Arts — 3

    Kindergarten — 6

    Grade 1 — 20

    Grade 2 — 37

    Blank - Ready for more activities — 55

Math — 57

    Kindergarten — 59

    Grade 1 — 65

    Grade 2 — 69

    Blank - Ready for more activities — 78

Science — 81

    Kindergarten — 84

    Grade 1 — 89

    Grade 2 — 95

    Blank - Ready for more activities — 101

History — 103

    Kindergarten — 116

    Grade 1 — 120

    Grade 2 — 127

    Blank - Ready for more activities — 132

INDEX	140
ORDER FORM	145
ACTIVITIES FORM	146

For workshops or presentations by Dr. Joni, contact Familly Friendly Schools:

Phone/Fax: 1-530-899-8423
www.familyfriendlyschools.com

ABOUT THE LEARNING STANDARDS

The standards used in the Parent Playbook series are a combination of Common Core and State Standards for English Language Arts and Math.

The standards used in this material are a representation of all State Learning Standards and are tested in every state.

The major purpose for use of the standards is to provide teachers and parents a guideline for skills taught at each grade level.

Standards for Science and Social Studies are tested in every state. Science and Social Studies activities for parents are included here and matched to a set of learning standards derived from across the United States.

We do hope these activities will be both enjoyable and filled with learning for both parents, teachers, and, most important, children.

ENGLISH LANGUAGE ARTS

K - 2

Parent Playbook Activities

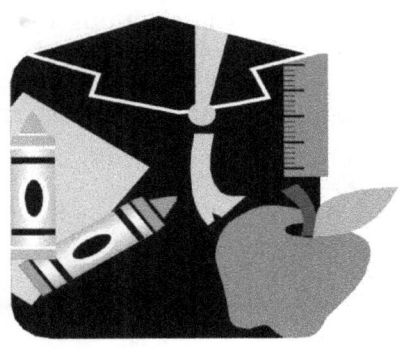

Want to add your favorite activity to the next Parent Playbook?
Use the convenient form in the back of this book or contact the publisher at:

www.familyfriendlyschools.com • www.engagepress.com

By Dr. Joni Samples   English Language Arts Learning Standards

ENGLISH LANGUAGE ARTS LEARNING STANDARDS
Grades K-2

The purpose for English Language Arts (ELA) Standards is to guarantee that all students develop the language skills they need to succeed in life as informed, productive members of society.

The ability to read and write begins before children enter school as they experience and experiment with language activities – from babbling to learning sounds and words.

Children begin to make connections between reading, writing, speaking, and listening as a way of gathering information and learning about the world around them.

The ELA Standards are listed on the following page to help you understand and put together all the skills needed to read and write. No standard stands alone. They all work together to create a language arts program.

Basic Topics of the English Language Arts Learning Standards - Grades K-2

Reading Standards for Literature
    Key Ideas and Details
    Craft and Structure
    Integration of Knowledge and Ideas
    Range of Reading and Level of Text Complexity

Reading Standards for Informational Text
    Key Ideas and Details
    Craft and Structure
    Integration of Knowledge and Ideas
    Range of Reading and Level of Text Complexity

Reading Standards Foundational Skills
    Phonics and Word Recognition
    Fluency

Writing Standard
    Text Types and Purposes
    Production and Distribution of Writing
    Research to Build and Present Knowledge
    Range of Writing

Speaking and Listening Standard
    Comprehension and Collaboration
    Presentation and Knowledge of Ideas

Language Standard
    Conventions of Standard English
    Knowledge of Language
    Vocabulary Acquisition and Use

Story Time
Number of People: 2   Time: Varies

Grade Level **K**

Materials: Favorite stories

Anytime can be story time. One of my favorite time for telling a story is the evening, before bedtime. A short story every evening helps a child learn language, new words, and the flow and structure of a story. If it's the same story, don't be surprised to hear it told back to you after a few readings.

ENGLISH LANGUAGE ARTS STANDARD

Reading Standards for Literature: Key Ideas and Details

1. With prompting and support, ask and answer questions about details and events in a text.

Beginning to Read Aloud
Number of People: 1+   Time: 10-20 minutes

Grade Level **K**

Materials: Books

Description: Reading aloud to children helps them become successful readers. Choose books that are too easy to read rather than too hard. Books with lots of pictures and just a few words are good starters. You read the book aloud first pointing to each word, then read the book out loud again together pointing to each word. They'll be ready to take over and re-tell or "read" it to you when the confidence is there. Let them do it. They will soon have a favorite book and know every word by heart. You won't be able to skip a page without them knowing it. They want to be successful in this new skill.

ENGLISH LANGUAGE ARTS STANDARD

Reading Standards for Literature: Key Ideas and Details

2. With prompting and support, retell familiar stories, including key details.

You could write "a STARfish is a wonderful friend."

Rebus Writing

Number of People: 1 Time: 15-30 minutes Grade Level: **K**

Materials: Paper, pencil, crayons or pictures from magazines

Description: Write a story then replace some of the words with pictures. For example, if you wrote "The horse jumped over the fence," the words "horse" and "fence" can be replaced with pictures. Help your child read the story with the pictures in it.

ENGLISH LANGUAGE ARTS STANDARD

Reading Standards for Literature: Integration of Knowledge and Ideas:

7. With prompting and support, describe the relationship between illustrations and the story in which they appear (e.g., what moment in a story an illustration depicts)

What we learned today...

_____

_____

_____

_____

_____

_____

Favorite Topics

Number of People: 2 Time: 15 minutes

Grade Level **K**

Materials: Books, magazine, or Internet article

Description: Choose a topic for the evening and read something about that topic. Maybe he likes cars or dinosaurs. Maybe she likes puppies or kitties. Choose a topic for the evening and read something about that topic. Just a short piece from a book, magazine or the Internet will do. After you have read the story, ask questions about the topic. What did we read about in the story? What were the main things he/she heard? Try to have your child identify one or two details.

ENGLISH LANGUAGE ARTS STANDARD

Reading: Informational Text: Key Ideas and Details

2. With prompting and support, identify the main topic and retell key details of a text.

What we learned today...

_____

_____

_____

_____

_____

_____

Write Right

Number of People: 2   Time: 15 minutes

Grade Level **K**

Materials: Paper and pencil, crayon, or marker

Description: Using small, medium or large a piece of paper and a marker of some sort, have your child "write" a story beginning in the upper left hand corner. The story can be just a few letters, squiggles, or pictures—it doesn't matter. The purpose of this activity is to have the story go from *left to right*. The child starts in the upper left and moves to the right on the paper. Once a "line" of the story is filled, he goes back to the left side and continues with the story moving to the right side of the page. You may need a large area to display the number of stories written, but it will be worth it.

ENGLISH LANGUAGE ARTS STANDARD

Reading Skills: Foundational Skills: Print Concepts

1a. Follow words from left to right, top to bottom, and page by page.

Double Duty Bookmarks

Number of People: 1+   Time: 15-20 minutes

Grade Level **K**

Materials: Books, bookmark

Description: For young readers, a bookmark can hold a place and it can also be used under sentences to help a child track the sentence. Don't worry, they'll give it up when it begins to slow them down.

ENGLISH LANGUAGE ARTS STANDARD

Reading Standards: Foundational Skills: Print Concepts

1a. Follow words from left to right, top to bottom, and page by page.

While Reading the Newspaper

Number of People: 2 Time: 10 minutes Grade Level **K**

Materials: Newspaper

Description: Newspapers have headlines with very large letters. Pointing to the letters and having your child identify the letter or tell you the sound the letter makes, is good reinforcement for your new reader.

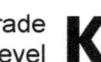

ENGLISH LANGUAGE ARTS STANDARD

Reading Standards: Foundational Skills: Print Concepts

1b. Recognize that spoken words are represented in written language by specific sequences of letters.

Alphabet Fun

Number of People: 1+ Time: 10-20 minutes Grade Level **K**

Materials: Small sticky notes, pen or pencil

Description: A great opportunity to teach letters is while you're fixing dinner. Place a pad of sticky notes and a pen or pencil next to the stove. Write one letter on a yellow sticky note. Ask your child to tell you the name of the letter. Then ask your child to find something in the room that starts with that letter. He can stick the note on to the item when he finds it. Variations: Rather than concentrate on the name of a letter, you can concentrate on sound of the letter. With a more experienced reader, you can say a word and then have your child find the letter that begins that word.

ENGLISH LANGUAGE ARTS STANDARD

Reading Standards: Foundational Skills: Print Concepts

1d. Recognize and name all upper– and lowercase letters of the alphabet.

Alphabet Game

Number of People: 1+   Time: 10-20 minutes

Grade Level **K**

Materials: none

Description: Searching for letters is always a fun game. Look for signs along the road and point out the first letters in a word going in order from A to Z. For instance, 'A' for a sign with 'Avenue' then 'B' for a sign with the word 'Beach'. Try it backwards too.

ENGLISH LANGUAGE ARTS STANDARD

Reading Standards: Foundational Skills: Print Concepts

1d. Recognize and name all upper– and lowercase letters of the alphabet.

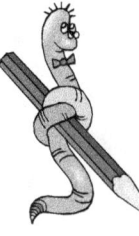

What we learned today...

_____

_____

_____

_____

_____

Keyboard Letters

Number of People: 1+   Time: 10-20 minutes

Grade Level

Materials: Picture of a computer keyboard with letters on the keys

Description: Download a picture of a computer keyboard. It has all the letters of the alphabet. While you're working on your computer, let your child color the keyboard letters of her name in the picture. Have her say the letters as she colors them. Make several copies and let her color other simple words using the keyboard letters.

ENGLISH LANGUAGE ARTS STANDARD

Reading Standards: Foundational Skills: Print Concepts
1d. Recognize and name all upper– and lowercase letters of the alphabet.

What we learned today...

_____

_____

_____

_____

_____

_____

Rhymes

Number of People: 2+   Time: varies   Grade Level **K**

Materials: Car

Description: Pick a word while you're driving to town. Have your children think of as many words as they can to rhyme with it before you reach your first destination. Pick another word before you get to the second stop.

ENGLISH LANGUAGE ARTS STANDARD

Reading Standards: Foundational Skills: Phonological Awareness

2a. Recite and produce rhyming words.

Rhyme Time

Number of People: 2   Time: 15 minutes   Grade Level **K**

Materials: None

Description: There are several kinds of rhyming games. One version is to give your child two words and let him tell you whether they rhyme or not. Then the child can give you two words and you say if it rhymes or not. Go back and forth. Another version is "Odd-one-Out". Give the child three words, two that rhyme and one that doesn't. Let the child tell you the one that doesn't rhyme. Make it a bedtime ritual along with a favorite story. You'll both have fun.

ENGLISH LANGUAGE ARTS STANDARD

Reading Standards: Foundational Skills: Phonological Awareness

2.a. Recognize and produce rhyming words.

Computer Letters

Number of People: 2+   Time: 10-20 min   Grade Level: **K**

Materials: Computer Keyboard

Description: Save a keyboard from a discarded computer. While you work on your computer, let your child practice letter-sound recognition on his keyboard. Ask: Where's the letter that sounds like "tee"? Find the "fuh" sound. What letter sounds like "mmm"? If you can manage to set up an entire computer system with a monitor for him, he will see the letters on the screen as he hits them.

ENGLISH LANGUAGE ARTS STANDARD

Reading Standards: Foundation Skills: Phonics and Word Recognition

3a. Demonstrate basic knowledge of one-to-one letter-sound correspondences by producing the primary or many of the most frequent sound for each consonant.

Word Families

Number of People: 2   Time: 15 minutes   Grade Level: **K**

Materials: Paper and pencil

Description: Some words come in sets. Words like cat, hat, fat, mat, and sat are in the "at" family. Write

        __at

on a piece of paper. Have your child write the first letter of the words that belong in that family. Have him say or write as many words as he can from that family. Then change families. Try the '-et', '-ig', '-op', or any number of vowel-consonant families (sets). This is fun for writing and helps with reading too.

ENGLISH LANGUAGE ARTS STANDARD

Reading Standards: Foundational Skills: Phonics and Word Recognition

3d. Distinguish between similarly spelled words by identifying the sounds of the letters that differ.

Learning to Read Comes in Steps	Grade Level **K**
Number of People: 2 Time: Minutes to an hour	

Materials: None; need just a great deal of talking and listening

Description: Just like a child can learn to talk by going from babbling to complete sentences, a child learns to read in stages too. They hear sounds first but it's more fun when the sounds come together to make meaningful words. Later, those words join together to form a message.

Reading starts by listening and then by speaking coherently. Support them as they go—they need feedback but not strong correction. Practice, practice, practice—the more they read the better readers they'll become. You can help. Model by reading yourself — children like to do what those around them are doing.

ENGLISH LANGUAGE ARTS STANDARD

Reading Standards: Foundational Skills: Fluency

4. Read emergent-reader texts with purpose and understanding.

What we learned today...

_____

_____

_____

_____

_____

_____

Tell Me A Story

Number of People: 2   Time: 10 minutes

Grade Level **K**

Materials: Paper and pencil

Description: Have your child write a story just for you. Let him spell whatever words he can. Sometimes the letters won't look like letters, but the writing and the story will be his. As he gets older and more experienced, he'll straighten out the letters and the words.

ENGLISH LANGUAGE ARTS STANDARD

Writing Standards: Text Types and Purposes

3. Use a combination of drawing, dictating, and writing to narrate a single event or several loosely linked events, tell about the events in the order that they occurred, and provide a reaction to what happened.

What we learned today...

_____

_____

_____

_____

_____

_____

Stories Out Loud

Number of People: 2+   Time: 20 minutes

Grade Level **K**

Materials: None

Description: Have your child recall a book he's read or have him remember an experience of any kind that he has had. Once he is ready, listen to him talk about his book or explain his experience. When he is finished ask him questions. This is great preparation for learning organizational skills, sequencing, memory, and more.

ENGLISH LANGUAGE ARTS STANDARD

Speaking and Listening Standard: Comprehension and Collaboration

3. Ask and answer question in order to seek help, get information or clarify something that is not understood.

Stories to Tell

Number of People: 1+   Time: 15-30 minutes

Grade Level **K**

Materials: Paper, pencil

Description: Have your child make up a story and then tell an adult. The adult writes the story. Let your child act out the story.

ENGLISH LANGUAGE ARTS STANDARD

Speaking and Listening Standards: Presentation of Knowledge and Ideas

4. Describe familiar people, place, things, and events and, with prompting and support, provide additional detail.

Alphabet Write

Number of People: 1+   Time: 10-20 minutes   Grade Level **K**

Materials: Paper, pencil

Description: Have your child sit at the dinner table while you're fixing dinner and write the letters of the alphabet. He can do all uppercase, then all lowercase or all the ones he knows. Work on the formation of the letters as well as the spacing.

ENGLISH LANGUAGE ARTS STANDARD

Language Standards: Conventions in Writing and Speaking

1. a. Print most upper– and lower case letters.

Catalog Trails

Number of People: 1   Time: 10-20 minutes   Grade Level **K**

Materials: Mail order catalog or a newspaper

Description: Mail order catalogs come into most homes. A newspaper also has a pull-out section with a variety of pictures of merchandise. Let your child go through and pick out the items she likes. Have her circle her favorite items then describe them to you. This activity is good for vocabulary and great for you to know what to do about holidays and birthdays.

ENGLISH LANGUAGE ARTS STANDARD

Language Standard: Vocabulary Acquisition and Use

5a. Sort common objects into categories to gain a sense of the concepts the categories represent.

It's too bad you don't usually see a STARfish on the road.

Travel Game

Number of People: 1+ Time: Trip length Grade Level: K

Materials: Car, list of things found on the road side

Description: Make a list of things to find while on the road—a red truck, a barn, pizza sign, license plate from Oregon, etc. How many can you find? Have your child describe each item as she sees it.

ENGLISH LANGUAGE ARTS STANDARD

Language Standards: Vocabulary Acquisition and Use

5c. Identify real-life connections between words and their use.

What we learned today...

_____

_____

_____

_____

_____

_____

Stick It Notes

Number of People: 2 Time: 15 minutes Grade Level **1**

Materials: Computers

Description: Many computers have a sticky note function. Use the sticky note function to ask a few questions of your child after you've read a story. See what responses you get back. Start your notes with: who, what, when, where and how.

ENGLISH LANGUAGE ARTS STANDARD

Reading Standards for Literature: Key Ideas and Details

1. Ask and answer questions about key details and events in a text.

What we learned today...

_____

_____

_____

_____

_____

_____

Stories Out Loud 2
Number of People: 2+   Time: 20 minutes   Grade Level **1**

Materials: None

Description: Yes, we've done this before, but this year it will work even better. Have your child recall a book he's read or have him remember an experience of any kind. Once he is ready, listen to him explain his book or experience. When he is finished, ask him questions (What happened in the story? What was your favorite part? Who did you like best in the story?) This is great preparation for organizational skills, sequencing, memory, and more.

ENGLISH LANGUAGE ARTS STANDARD

Reading Standards for Literature: Key Ideas and Details

2. Retail stories, including key details, and demonstrate understanding of their central message or lesson.

Who Tells it?
Number of People: 1+   Time: 10-20 minutes   Grade Level **1**

Materials: Book

Description: Read a favorite story and every once in a while ask who's telling the story. Is it Christopher Robin? Winnie the Pooh? Or is someone else telling the story? Ask the same question with a new story.

ENGLISH LANGUAGE ARTS STANDARD

Reading: Literature

6. Identify who is telling the story at various points in a text.

Book Club

Number of People: 2+   Time: 15-30 minutes   Grade Level 1

Materials: Favorite books

Description: In a book club, the members all read the same book and discuss it. This "Book Club" isn't any different. You read the same book your child is reading, but in a different version. When you both finish, discuss the book together. What's the story about? Who was your favorite character? Part way through the book, talk about how he thinks it will end. Talk about the ways the story is the same and different in each version.

ENGLISH LANGUAGE ARTS STANDARD

Reading Standards for Literature: Integration of Knowledge and Ideas

9. Compare and contrast the adventures and experiences of characters in stories.

Read Aloud

Number of People: 2   Time: Varies   Grade Level 1

Materials: Book

Description: Have your child read to you while you are driving to the grocery store. Just be sure the book is easy enough to read. You wouldn't want to have her get stuck on a word like 'supercalifragilistic' or by the time she gets to 'expealidocious' you may be driving on the sidewalk.

ENGLISH LANGUAGE ARTS STANDARD

Reading Standards for Literature: Range and Level of Text Complexity

10. With prompting and support, read prose and poetry of appropriate complexity for grade 1.

How many STARs can you find in the grocery store?

Grocery List
Number of People: 1+   Time: 10-20 minutes

Grade Level **1**

Materials: Grocery store, grocery list
Description: When you go to the store, show your child three items on the grocery list. Ask him to find them. This activity is good for reading and learning to follow directions.

ENGLISH LANGUAGE ARTS STANDARD

Reading Standards for Informational Text: Craft and Structure

4. Ask and answer question to help determine or clarify the meaning of words and phrases in a text.

What we learned today...

_____

_____

_____

_____

_____

_____

_____

Don't forget to STARt a sentence with a capital letter.

Sentence Scramble
Number of People: 2   Time: 10 minutes

Grade Level **1**

Materials: Small pieces of paper or index cards; pencil

Description: While you're scrambling eggs in the kitchen your child can unscramble sentences. Make a list of short sentences. Let her see one of the sentences and read it with you. Write the sentence on a strip of paper and cut the words apart. Then have her turn around while you mix up the words in the sentence. Then have her put the words in the right order. When you finish one sentence, try another. Don't forget capitals and periods. Have her read the sentences during breakfast.

ENGLISH LANGUAGE ARTS STANDARD

Reading Standards: Foundational Skills

1a. Recognize the distinguish features of a sentence (e.g. first word, capitalization, ending punctuation.

What we learned today...

___
___
___
___
___
___

Word Groups

Number of People: 2   Time: 15 minutes

Grade Level **1**

Materials: Paper and pencil or you can do this aloud

Description: Word families (or sets) with blending sounds (two letters that make one sound) can make for an interesting time. The "at" family is a good one to start with. How many words can your child make adding at least two letters with the end letters "__at" that add 'br' to make 'brat' or 'dr' to make 'drat' or 'sp' to make 'splat'. Who can make the most words? Try "-ar", "-et", "-ay". There are many others.

ENGLISH LANGUAGE ARTS STANDARD

Reading Standards: Foundational Skills

2b. Orally produce single-syllable words by blending phonemes, including consonant blends

Word Hunt

Number of People: 1+   Time: 10-20 minutes

Grade Level **1**

Materials: Small sticky notes

Description: Write the name of an object in a room of the house on a sticky note. Stick the names of the objects you've written on the objects in the room. Mix them up for fun. Put the sticky note for lamp on the desk or the sticky note for computer on the window. Ask your child to match the name with the correct object.

ENGLISH LANGUAGE ARTS STANDARD

Reading Standards: Foundational Skills: Phonics and Word Recognition

3. Know and apply grade-level phonics and word analysis skills in decoding words.

Find The Words
Number of People: 1+   Time: 10-20 minutes   Grade Level 1

Materials: Paper, pencil

Description: Write a large word like 'Halloween' or 'Thanksgiving' on a piece of paper. Let your kids see how many words they can make out of the letters in the word. Add another rule: the letters all have to be in the order they appear in the word. "Hall", "own", and "we" would count in the word 'Halloween'. "Won" wouldn't count since the letters are out of order. You can play this game with or without the rule.

ENGLISH LANGUAGE ARTS STANDARD

Reading Standards: Foundational Skills

3. Know and apply grade-level phonics and word analysis skills in decoding words.

Vocab Bingo
Number of People: 1+   Time: 15-30 minutes   Grade Level 1

Materials: Bingo type card with words in the squares, beans, M & M®s

Description: Use a bingo-type card, but replace the numbers with words from your child's reading book. Common sight words are especially helpful like: the, have, said, come, give, of. Put the same words on small slips of paper. Pull the words out of a bowl one at a time saying each word as you choose it. Have your child cover the word on his card as it is called. He can cover it with a bean or an M&M. Five across, down, or diagonal is a win. If you use M&M's, you might even let them eat the row when they win.

ENGLISH LANGUAGE ARTS STANDARD

Reading Standards: Foundational Skills: Phonics and Word Recognition

3. Know and apply grade-level phonics and word analysis skills in decoding words.

Can you find a STARfish at the bottom of your bowl?

Breakfast Read

Number of People: 1+   Time: 15 minutes

Grade Level **1**

Materials: Placemats, bowls, cereal boxes with words on them
Description: Placemats with letters on them, bowls with messages on the bottom, cereal boxes with stories or cereal in the shape of letters can be great teaching tools. Say the sounds of a letter and a part of word aloud then have your child find it in the cereal or on the placemat.

ENGLISH LANGUAGE ARTS STANDARD
Reading Standards: Foundational Skills: Print Concepts
3a. Know the spelling-sound correspondences for common consonant digraphs.

What we learned today...

_____

_____

_____

_____

_____

_____

Hard Words

Number of People: 1+   **Time:** 10-20 minutes

Grade Level 1

Materials: Something to read

Description: There are a variety of ways kids go about figuring out a new word. They might sound it out using letter sounds as clues. They can use the picture as a clue. They could skip over the word and come back to see what makes sense within the content of the writing. They might guess a word that would make sense, or they might start over again. It will probably take only a few seconds to find the clue that will bring the child to the right word. He will often get it given a little time. If he gets stuck you may have to help. You will have to find a balance between helping too soon and waiting so long that your child becomes frustrated. You know your child. Support him as he reads and he'll be fine.

ENGLISH LANGUAGE ARTS STANDARD

Reading Foundational Skills: Foundation Skills: Fluency

4. Read with sufficient accuracy and fluency to support comprehension.

What we learned today...

_____

_____

_____

_____

_____

_____

_____

My Words

Number of People: 2   Time: 5 minutes   Grade Level 1

Materials: Word magnets on a refrigerator

Description: Several sets of word magnets are available in stores these days. I have several of them. Use the words to write a sentence on the refrigerator every morning. When she comes in for breakfast, she can read her sentence aloud. "What do you want for breakfast?" "It is going to be hot today" "What will you do after school?" She'll look forward to finding out what the sentence for the day is.

ENGLISH LANGUAGE ARTS STANDARD

Reading Standards: Foundational Skills

4a. Read on-level text with purpose and understanding.

Sentence Rearranged

Number of People: 2   Time: 10 minutes   Grade Level 1

Materials: Strips of paper, pencil, scissors

Description: Have your child tell you a sentence. It could be about anything—a favorite pet, a birthday party, or anything of interest. Write the sentence down on a strip of paper. Then cut the strip into the words in the sentence. Let your child put all the words back in order and read the sentence aloud.

ENGLISH LANGUAGE ARTS STANDARD

Reading Standards: Foundational Skills

4c. Use context to confirm or self-correct word recognition and understanding, rereading as necessary.

What Is It?

Number of People: 2   Time: 20 minutes

Grade Level **1**

Materials: Paper and pencil

Description: Ask your child to write a description of something you can guess. Have her include hints about the object. After she has finished, have her read what she's written as you try to guess the object. If you can't guess what it is, have her write another sentence with another clue.

ENGLISH LANGUAGE ARTS STANDARD

Writing Standards: Text Types and Purposes

1. Write opinion pieces in which they introduce the topic or name the book they are writing about, state an opinion, supply a reason for the opinion and provide some sense of closure.

Write Focus

Number of People: 2   Time: 15 minutes

Grade Level **1**

Materials: Paper and pencil, one object

Description: Choose one of your child's favorite objects—a rock, a shell, a doll, or a toy. Put the object on the table in front of him and ask him to write a sentence about it. You can help with spelling if he needs it. If he is just beginning to write, an alphabet chart may help. Have him read the sentence aloud when he finishes.

ENGLISH LANGUAGE ARTS STANDARD

Writing Standards

2. Write informative/explanatory texts in which they name a topic, supply some facts relevant to the topic, and provide some sense of closure.

STARt looking for letters and words.

Car Game(s)
Number of People: 1+   Time: Trip length

Grade Level **1**

Materials: Car, list of things found on the road side

Description: Car rides are great times for lots of learning to occur. Have your list of things to look for while on the way to market or to grandparents. You can look for letters, words or objects. Finding the letters of the alphabet in order is always fun. Can he find words on signs that start with the letter T? If it's objects you've asked for, there needs to be a complete description of the object so you know it's been spotted.

ENGLISH LANGUAGE ARTS STANDARD

Speaking and Listening Standards: Presentation of Knowledge and Ideas
1. Participate in collaborative conversations with diverse partners about grade 1 topics and texts with peers and adults in small and larger groups.

What we learned today...

_____

_____

_____

_____

_____

_____

Do you know any stories about STARfish?

Books on Tape
Number of People: 1+   Time: 10-20 minutes   Grade Level **1**

Materials: Books, tape-recorder, tapes
Description: Kids love to listen to stories. During story reading sessions, tape-record your child's favorite stories as you read them. He'll be able to play them at bedtime when you can't be there. Smart phones and iPads® now have this capability. At the end of the story, ask questions you can talk about later. Just don't forget to talk.

ENGLISH LANGUAGE ARTS STANDARD
Speaking and Listening Standards:
2. Ask and answer questions about key details in a text read aloud or information presented orally or through other media.

What we learned today...

_____

_____

_____

_____

_____

_____

TV Watching
Number of People: 2   Time: 5 minutes   Grade Level **1**

Materials: TV
Description: Make TV watching valuable. At the commercial break, ask your child what has happened so far. What does he think will happen next? What other way might the story end? Language development and thinking skills can be built along with the entertainment of the show.

ENGLISH LANGUAGE ARTS STANDARD
Speaking and Listening Standards
3. Ask and answer question about what a speaker says in order to gather additional information or clarify something that is not understood.

Magazine Book
Number of People: 1+   Time: 10-20 minutes   Grade Level **1**

Materials: Paper, magazines, scissors, glue
Description: Staple or tape several blank pieces of paper together to form a book. Then have your child cut pictures from a magazine to paste into her book. Designate each page as a display for a group of similar items. For example, put cars on page one, boats on page two, computers on page three and so on. She can describe each of the pages when she's ready.

ENGLISH LANGUAGE ARTS STANDARD
Speaking and Listening Standard: Presentation of Knowledge and Ideas
4. Describe people, places, things, and events with relevant details, expressing ideas and feelings clearly.

Alpha Write

Number of People: 1+   Time: 10-20 min

Grade Level **1**

Materials: Paper and pencil

Description: Lots of practice writing letters helps both writing and reading skills. There is plenty of time for practice while you go about routine chores. For instance, you can have your child practice writing letters while dinner is being fixed, when you're doing the laundry, or when you're dusting. Have your child write both capital and small letters.

ENGLISH LANGUAGE ARTS STANDARD

Language: Conventions of Standard English

1a. Print all upper– and lowercase letters.

Today, Tomorrow, and Yesterday

Number of People: 1+   Time: 10-20 min

Grade Level **1**

Materials: none

Description: Have your child describe his day. Then ask a question. What happened on that day at school? Example: I played ball at recess; What happened yesterday? Example: I played outside; What will you do tomorrow? I will go to Mary's birthday party.

ENGLISH LANGUAGE ARTS STANDARD

Language: Conventions of Standard English

1e. Use verbs to convey a sense of past, present..

Who Do You Know?

Number of People: 2 Time: 15 minutes

Grade Level **1**

Materials: None

Description: Play a game of who do you know. How many people do you and your child know that you can put on a list? First and last names if you can remember them. Make sure the first letters of each name are capitalized. Now think of more names for your list.

ENGLISH LANGUAGE ARTS STANDARD

Language: Conventions of Standard English

2a. Capitalize dates and names of people.

What we learned today...

_____

_____

_____

_____

_____

_____

Try making the word STAR in Word World.

Word World
Number of People: 1+   Time: 10-20 min

Grade Level 1

Materials: Books

Description: WordWorld™ on both TV and the Internet are great ways to play with words. If you've never seen a sheep made out of the letters s-h-e-e and p, you haven't seen WordWorld. There are a variety of games to play on the Internet site. A favorite is finding the words that fill in the blanks from several choices of the letter made animals and objects. Try it tonight!

ENGLISH LANGUAGE ARTS STANDARD

Language: Vocabulary Acquisition and Use
4a. Use sentence-level context as a clue.

What we learned today...

_____
_____
_____
_____
_____
_____

Retell 2
Number of People: 2   Time: 15 minutes

Grade Level **2**

Materials: Book (if needed)

Description: Your child has some favorite stories. Have him retell those stories to you. If he can't think of one, pick one to read aloud and then have him tell you the story he just heard. Ask questions so you won't miss any details of the story.

ENGLISH LANGUAGE ARTS STANDARD

Reading Standards for Literature: Key Ideas and Details

1. Ask and answer such questions as who, what, where, when why, and how to demonstrate understanding of key details in a text.

Make Reading Fun
Number of People: 1+   Time: 10-20 minutes

Grade Level **2**

Materials: Books

Description: Here are some ideas for making reading fun:
- On Friday or Saturday, plan a late bedtime so everyone can read a story or fable in bed before they go to sleep.
- On a rainy night, provide everyone with flashlights and let them read for an hour, then retell their story.
- One night a week at dinner have everyone share what story they are reading and what it means
- Set up a tent outside just for quiet reading time.

ENGLISH LANGUAGE ARTS STANDARD

Reading Standards for Literature: Key Ideas and Details

2. Recount stories, including fables and folktales from diverse cultures, and determine their central message, lesson, or moral.

Read Aloud 2

Number of People: 2　　Time: Varies　　Grade Level **2**

Materials: Book

Description: The car is such a great opportunity for reading time. Have your child read aloud to you in the car while you're driving to the grocery store, mall or just about anywhere. Talk about the way the story goes together and how it ends.

ENGLISH LANGUAGE ARTS STANDARD

Reading Standards for Literature: Key Ideas and Details

5. Describe the overall structure of a story, including describing how the beginning introduces the story and the ending concludes the action.

Story and Video

Number of People: 2　　Time: Varies　　Grade Level **2**

Materials: A movie made from a book & the book which the movie was made from

Description: My son's teacher showed the video "James and the Giant Peach." He came home talking so positively about the film, we checked the book out of the library and the video from the store. After reading a few chapters, we would stop reading and watch some of the video. Then we'd discuss the differences between the book and video. Try this with your child this evening.

ENGLISH LANGUAGE ARTS STANDARD

Reading Standards or Literature: Craft and Structure

9. Compare and contrast two or more versions of the same story (e.g., Cinderella stories) by different authors or from different cultures.

He'll be STARtled if you throw a sock at him!

Wash Day Read Aloud
Number of People: 2   Time: 15 minutes

Grade Level **2**

Materials: Book

Description: Have your beginning reader read to you while you're sorting the laundry. If he has trouble with a word you can always sock it to him.

ENGLISH LANGUAGE ARTS STANDARD

Reading Standards for Literature: Range and Level of Text Complexity

10. By the end of the year, read and comprehend literature, including stories and poetry, in the grades 2-3 text complexity band proficiently with scaffolding as needed at the high end of the range.

What we learned today...

_____

_____

_____

_____

_____

_____

STARt thinking of questions about your stories.

20 WWWWH Questions
Number of People: 2   Time: 15 minutes

Grade Level **2**

Materials: Favorite stories

Description: After you and your child have finished something fun to read, ask questions. Start your questions with: who, what, when, where and how. Who was your favorite character? What did he/she do? When did this story happen? See what kind of answers you get.

ENGLISH LANGUAGE ARTS STANDARD

Reading Standards for Informational Text: Key Ideas and Details

1. Ask and answer such questions as who, what, where, when, why, and how to demonstrate understanding of key details in a text.

_____

_____

_____

_____

_____

_____

Page 40

Noted Fun

Number of People: 2   Time: 20 minutes

Grade Level **2**

Materials: Paper, pencil

Description: On a day you need to be out of town, leave notes around for your child to read. Leave them on the breakfast table, in his lunchbox, in a coat pocket, on the mirror in the bathroom. Some can be directions or instructions, and some can just be funny notes. It's fun for him and you won't feel so guilty about being away.

ENGLISH LANGUAGE ARTS STANDARD

Reading Standards for Informational Text: Craft and Structure

6. Identify the main purpose of a text, including what question the author aims to answer or what the author aims to answer, explain or describe.

Read It to Me Again

Number of People: 2   Time: 15 minutes

Grade Level **2**

Materials: Favorite book and dirty dishes

Description: While you're doing dishes and listening to your child read, check to see if your child understands what's happening in the story. You won't have to stop the dishes. Just ask him a question and have him reread the part about "Goldilocks finding the three bowls." If he understands the story, he'll be able to find the part easily enough, and you can hear your favorite parts again. Ask him to read other stories, like his favorites by different authors. Talk about how they are the same and different.

ENGLISH LANGUAGE ARTS STANDARD

Reading Standards for Informational Text: Key Ideas and Details

9. Compare and contrast the most important points presented by two texts on the same topic.

 You are a STAR reader.

Reading a Magazine
Number of People: 2   Time: 10-20 mins

Grade Level **2**

Materials: Magazine at child's level

Description: Have your child help you read a magazine article. Depending on how advanced a reader she is, let her read aloud the words she knows, or read the first sentence and you read the rest, or you trade reading paragraphs. This activity lets you share your reading time with your child.

ENGLISH LANGUAGE ARTS STANDARD
Reading Standards for Informational Text
10. By the end of year, read and comprehend informational texts, including history/social studies, science, and technical texts, in the grades 2-3 text complexity band proficiently, with scaffolding is needed at the high end of the range.

_____

_____

_____

_____

_____

_____

Hard Words

Number of People: 1+ **Time:** 10-20 min **Grade Level:** 2

Materials: Something to read

Description: We've done this before, but it's important to know this year too. There are a variety of ways kids go about figuring out a new word. They might sound it out using letter sounds as clues. Pictures provide an idea. They could skip over the word and come back to see what makes sense within they read the sentence again. They might guess a word that would make sense, or they might start over again. It will probably take only a few seconds to find the clue that will bring the child to the right word. He will often get it given a little time. If he gets stuck you may have to help. There's a balance between helping too soon and waiting so long that your child becomes frustrated. You know your child. Support her as she reads. She'll be fine.

ENGLISH LANGUAGE ARTS STANDARD

Reading Standards: Foundational Skills: Phonics and Word Recognition

3. Know and apply grade-level phonics and word analysis skills in decoding words.

Missing Letters

Number of People: 1+ **Time:** 10-20 min **Grade Level:** 2

Materials: Chalk or whiteboard, chalk or marker, eraser

Description: Having a chalkboard or whiteboard in your kitchen allows you to spend time doing skills with your kids while you prepare meals. Have them write a sentence on the board then close their eyes. Then, while their eyes are closed, erase several letters and then have them uncover their eyes. Ask them to fill in the blanks. Or, you can replace the letters with incorrect letters and let them figure out which ones are wrong and correct them. (Don't forget to stir the soup).

ENGLISH LANGUAGE ARTS STANDARD

Reading Standards: Foundational Skills

3. Know and apply grade-level phonics and word analysis skills in decoding words.

Reading Buddies

Number of People: 2   Time: 15 minutes

Grade Level **2**

Materials: Books

Description: It may be hard to build in the extra reading time when you're busy, but there are others who can help. Let children read to grandmas, friends, neighbors, brothers, and sisters. When our girls were little and just starting to read, their brothers were older and read stories for school every day. It was also our rule that they read 100 pages a week before they were allowed to watch TV. The boys got extra credit for reading or retelling those stories aloud to their little sisters.

ENGLISH LANGUAGE ARTS STANDARD

Reading Standards Foundational Skills: Fluency

4. Read with sufficient accuracy and fluency to support comprehension

Exercise Your Child's Reading

Number of People: 1+   Time: 10-20 min

Grade Level **2**

Materials: Books

Description: As you spend 20 minutes on an exercise bike, let your child spend the time reading out loud to you. He gets to read and you don't have to count the seconds until you're through. As an alternate, let him read silently and tell you about the story.

ENGLISH LANGUAGE ARTS STANDARD

Reading Standards: Foundational Skills: Fluency

4. Read with sufficient accuracy and fluency to support comprehension.

You can STAR in your own stories.

My First...
Number of People: 2   Time: 20 minutes

Grade Level **2**

Materials: Paper and pencil or computer

Description: Often, a child needs a topic for writing. A blank sheet of paper is a scary thing for any writer. Children can often write for a long time when given something specific to write about. A simple start is a question: What's your favorite puppy, school activity, TV show, or who's your best friend? The question can be whatever you know will interest your child.

ENGLISH LANGUAGE ARTS STANDARD

Writing Standards: Text Types and Purposes

1. Write opinions in which they introduce the topic or book they are writing about, state an opinion, supply reasons that support the opinion, use linking words (e.g., because, and, also) to connect opinion and reasons, and provide a concluding statement or section.

What we learned today...

_____

_____

_____

_____

_____

_____

STARt up your hair dryer and STARt writing.

Dry it Write   Grade Level **2**
Number of People: 1+   Time: 10-20 mins

Materials: Paper, pencil

Description: It's too noisy for conversation while you're blow-drying your hair so let your child write you notes with lots of detail. Great for writing, spelling, and telling secrets.

ENGLISH LANGUAGE ARTS STANDARD

Writing Standards:Text Types and Purposes

2. Write informative/explanatory texts in which they introduce a topic, use facts and definitions to develop points, and provide a concluding statement or section.

___

___

___

___

___

___

Prompt Me

Number of People: 1   Time: 30 minutes

Grade Level **2**

Materials: Paper and pencil or a computer

Description: Give your child the first few words of a story or a topic then let him write whatever he likes. A prompt might be: "It was a dark and scary night…,"; "Last night my dog…"; "Friday after school, I…"; and on and on. This can be used at almost any age. If you start when your child is young and it becomes a game and a habit, you can be doing it until he finishes high school. You can also tie the activity into other classes, especially history.

ENGLISH LANGUAGE ARTS STANDARD

Writing Standards: Text Types and Purposes

3. Write narratives in which they recount a well-elaborated event or short sequence of events, include details to describe actions, thoughts, and feelings, use temporal words to signal event order, and provide a sense of closure.

Letters to Grandma

Number of People: 3   Time: 20 minutes

Grade Level **2**

Materials: Paper and pencil

Description: Letters are always fun to send and receive, and grandmas are usually great places to start. Let your child write a letter to grandma. Show him how to include the date (so she'll know when she wrote it), salutation ("Dear Grandma" tells her to whom it was written, body (what she wants to tell her), closing, (love), and the signature (this tells her who it's from). It may take some editing to get the entire letter right, but the finished product is worth it. Grandmas are good to write to because they usually write back.

ENGLISH LANGUAGE ARTS STANDARD

Writing Standard: Production and Distribution of Writing

5. With guidance and support from adults and peers, focus on a topic and strengthen writing as needed by revising and editing.

Writing Letters
Number of People: 2   Time: 30 minutes   Grade Level **2**

Materials: Paper and pencil

Description: While you're writing emails to friends, let your child write an email too. Sending emails to grandparents or cousins—someone who will write back—means a return email to read. This is great writing and reading reinforcement.

ENGLISH LANGUAGE ARTS STANDARD

Writing Standard: Production and Distribution of Writing

6. With guidance and support from adults, use a variety of digital tools to produce and publish writing, including in collaboration with peers.

Look It Up
Number of People: 2   Time: 30 minutes   Grade Level **2**

Materials: Dictionary, thesaurus, atlas

Description: The using of reference materials should start early. Ask your child to write a story about dinosaurs, or volcanoes, or outer space. Choose something she has an interest in but may not know well. Help her find what she wants to say in the right reference book--a dictionary, a thesaurus, an encyclopedia, an atlas or whatever it takes to find what you need.

ENGLISH LANGUAGE ARTS STANDARD

Writing Standards: Research to Build Knowledge

7. Participate in shared research and writing projects (e.g., read a number of books on a single topic to produce a report; record science observations).

Can't Get To The Bookstore

Number of People: 1+   Time: 10-20 mins

Grade Level **2**

Materials: Book Club offers

Description: Your child may bring home *Arrow, Scholastic*, or other book club offers from school. These companies offer cheap prices for great reading. If these publications are not available at your school try *www.amazon.com*. Once the books you have ordered arrive, spend time reading them together.

ENGLISH LANGUAGE ARTS STANDARD

Speaking and Listening Standards: Comprehensions and Collaboration

1. Participate in collaborative conversations with diverse partners about grade 2 topics and texts with peers and adults in small and larger groups.

_____

_____

_____

_____

_____

_____

 A book that STARs a hero is a great story.

Stories Out Loud-3
Number of People: 2+   Time: 20 mins   Grade Level **2**

Materials: None Needed

Description: And one more time, have your child remember a book he's read in his class or something he's learned at school. Once he is ready, listen to him explain his book or experience. When he is finished ask him questions. This is great preparation for organizational skills, sequencing, memory, and more.

ENGLISH LANGUAGE ARTS STANDARD

Speaking and Listening Standards: Comprehension and Collaboration

1c. Ask for clarification and further explanation as needed about the topics and texts under discussion.

_____
_____
_____
_____
_____
_____

Schedule It

Number of People: 2   Time: 15 minutes

Grade Level **2**

Materials: TV, TV guide

Description: Talk with your child about which programs to watch as you look at the TV schedule. Discuss the shows and what topics they cover. Circle the ones you and she want to see. This activity helps with listening, speaking, reading, the organizing of your time, and avoids the dreaded disease—channel surfing.

ENGLISH LANGUAGE ARTS STANDARD

Speaking and Listening Standard:

2. Recount or describe key ideas or details from a text read aloud or information presented orally or through other media.

TV Watching 2

Number of People: 2   Time: 5 minutes

Grade Level **2**

Materials: TV

Description: TV is a big part of our lives these days so let's continue to make it worthwhile. Choose only shows you want your child to watch and then ask questions about what is happening, what the characters are talking about, and the way the show might end. Talk during commercial breaks and before the end of the show. See if your predictions for an ending turn out to be correct.

ENGLISH LANGUAGE ARTS STANDARD

Speaking and Listening Standard:Comprehension and Collaboration

3. Ask and answer questions about what a speaker says in order to clarify comprehension, gather additional information, or deepen understanding of a topic or issue.

TV Listening
Number of People: 2   Time: 15 minutes

Grade Level **2**

Materials: Television show
Description: Here's another TV activity. If you have recording capabilities, record the show and watch half of it. Have your child tell you three possible ways the show could end. Pick your favorite ending then return to the show to see what really happens.

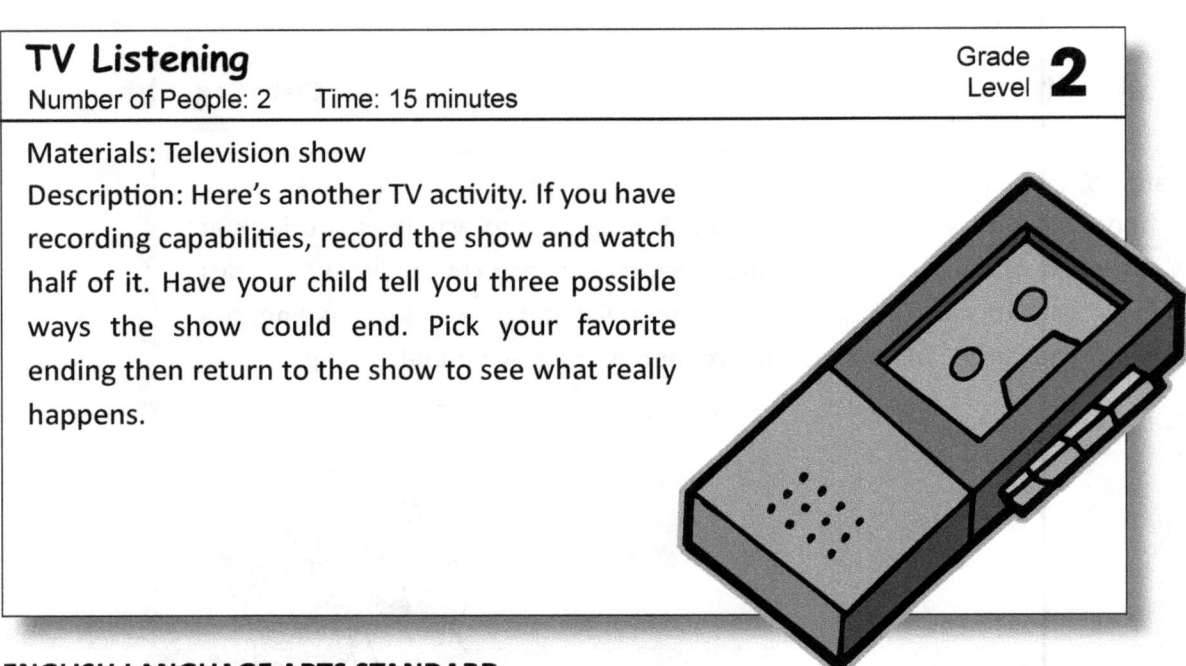

ENGLISH LANGUAGE ARTS STANDARD
Speaking and Listening Standards: Presentation of Knowledge and Ideas
4. Tell a story or recount an experience with appropriate facts and relevant, descriptive details, speaking audibly in coherent sentences.

Drawings Book
Number of People: 1+   Time: 10-20 minutes

Grade Level **2**

Materials: Paper, magazines, scissors, glue
Description: Staple or tape several blank pages together to make a book. Designate each page as a separate item. Have your child draw pictures on each page about a particular topic or series of topics. She can tell a story or relate an experience about the things she has drawn when she's ready.

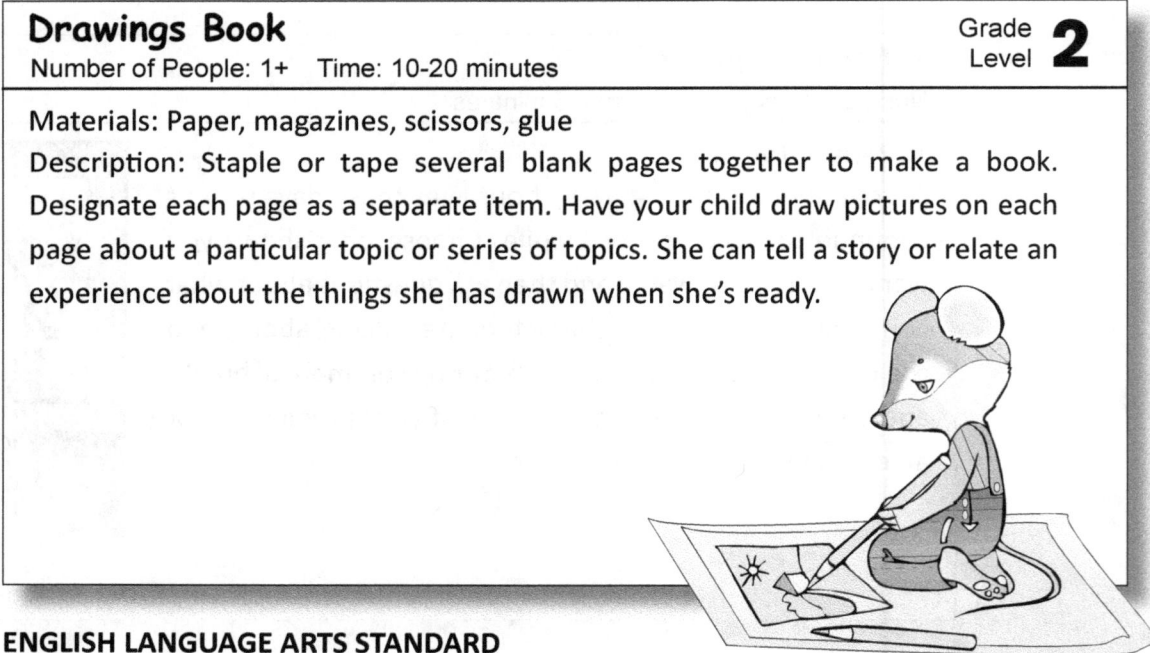

ENGLISH LANGUAGE ARTS STANDARD
Speaking and Listening Standards: Presentation of Knowledge and Ideas
5. Create audio recordings of stories or poems, add drawings or other visual displays to tell stories or recounts of experiences when appropriate to claify ideas, thoughts, and feelings.

Directions, Directions

Number of People: 2   Time: 20 minuntes

Grade Level **2**

Materials: Those items your child says you need

Description: Have your child give you directions. A fun way to do this one is to ask your child to tell you how to make a peanut butter sandwich. Tell her you are going to follow her directions exactly. As she tells you what to do, follow them. If she tells you to put peanut butter on the bread, do it. You may have to do it with your fingers if she doesn't tell you to use a knife. She'll figure out very quickly how important it is to give all the directions.

ENGLISH LANGUAGE ARTS STANDARD

Speaking and Listening Standards: Comprehensions and Collaboration

6. Produce complete sentences when appropriate to task and situation in order to provide requested detail or clarification.

 Let's see 6 for dinner. STARt counting.

Following Directions

Number of People: 2   Time: 15 minutes

Grade Level **2**

Materials: Dinner table

Description: You can turn preparation for mealtime into quite a bit more than just a chore. Ask your child to put the spoons on the table, put the glasses next to the plates, and the napkins on the plate. You can make up your own directions. You may not get the table set completely, but you will be having your child practice following three- and four-step oral directions. Do this every night and she'll become quite good at it.

ENGLISH LANGUAGE ARTS STANDARD

Language Standards: Vocabulary Acquisition and Use

5.a. Identify real-life connections between words and their use (e.g., describe foods that are spicy or juicy.)

Create your own playbook activities!

Language Arts
Number of People: Time: Grade Level

Materials:
Description:

ENGLISH LANGUAGE ARTS STANDARD

Language Arts
Number of People: Time: Grade Level

Materials:
Description:

ENGLISH LANGUAGE ARTS STANDARD

Create your own playbook activities!

Language Arts
Number of People: Time: Grade Level

Materials:
Description:

ENGLISH LANGUAGE ARTS STANDARD

Language Arts
Number of People: Time: Grade Level

Materials:
Description:

ENGLISH LANGUAGE ARTS STANDARD

MATH

K – 2

Parent Playbook Activities

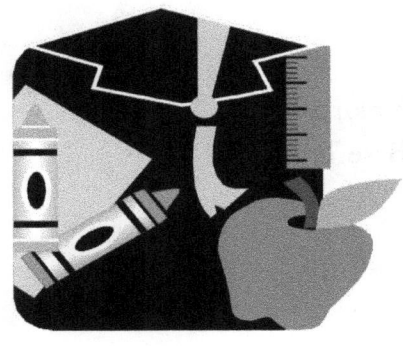

Want to add your favorite activity to the next Parent Playbook?
Use the convenient form in the back of this book or contact the publisher at:

www.familyfriendlyschools.com • www.engagepress.com

By Dr. Joni SamplesMath Learning Standards

MATH LEARNING STANDARDS
Grades K-2

Kindergarten
    Counting & Cardinality
    Operations & Algebraic Thinking
    Number & Base Operations in Ten
    Measurement & Data
    Geometry

Grade 1
    Operations & Algebraic Thinking
    Number & Operations in Base Ten
    Measurement & Data
    Geometry

Grade 2
    Operations & Algebraic Thinking
    Number & Operations in Base Ten
    Measurement & Data
    Geometry

Telephone Calls

Number of People: 2   Time: 10 minutes   Grade Level: K

Materials: Telephone

Description: It takes practice to learn how to use the telephone. Have your child call a relative. Dialing numbers in the correct order is a learned skill, and he will want to hear someone he knows answer. You don't want it to be an irate neighbor. Try another friend or relative. One number sequence is not the same as another.

MATH LEARNING STANDARD

Counting & Cardinality: Know number names and the count sequence

2. Count forward beginning from a given number within the known sequence (instead of having to begin at 1).

Breakfast Math

Number of People: 2 or more   Time: 20 minutes   Grade Level: K

Materials: Placemat with numbers and math facts on them

Description: We used placemats with pictures and numbers on them. For example, one placement has the number 5 with five cherries. Some placemats have addition problems, some subtraction, some multiplication, and some division. We got two sets of each. Depending on the age and skill of the child, each child had one under his plate with every meal. We'd take turns with each child identifying the numbers and solving the math problem.

MATH LEARNING STANDARD

Counting & Cardinality: Count to tell the number of objects

4b. Understand that the last number name said tells the number of objects counted. The number of objects is the same regardless of their arrangement or the order in which they were counted.

Operations & Algebraic Thinking:

5. Fluently add and subtract within 5.

License Number Recognition

Number of People: 2   Time: 15 minutes

Grade Level: **K**

Materials: Car

Description: While traveling, let your little ones see if they can identify the numbers on nearby car license plates. They can start with single digits, and then try double digits. Have older children add the digits together.

MATH LEARNING STANDARD

Counting & Cardinality: Compare Numbers

7. Compare two numbers between 1 and 10 presented as written numerals.

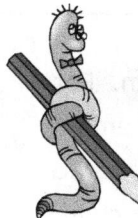

What we learned today...

_____

_____

_____

_____

_____

_____

War

Number of People: 2+   Time: 30 or + minutes   Grade Level **K**

Materials: Playing Cards

Description: The card game "War" is fun and helps young learners understand the concepts of greater than and less than. Split a deck of cards between the players. Players put their cards in a stack face down and turn up the top card. The player with the highest card wins all cards turned face up. The winner is the one with the most cards when all the cards have been turned face up.

MATH LEARNING STANDARD

Counting & Cardinality: Compare Numbers

6. Identify whether the number of objects in one group is greater than, less than, or equal to the number of objects in another group.

Garage Sort

Number of People: 2   Time: 20 minutes   Grade Level **K**

Materials: Items in the garage

Description: Your garage is a great place to start data collection and you may not even know it. There are screws and nails and other items that sometimes get mixed with each other. Let your kindergartener sort them out. Buttons in a button box can be sorted by color or texture. Sorting and classifying objects is a first stage to understanding algebra. Once the objects are sorted, have her count the items in the groups as high as she can count.

MATH LEARNING STANDARD

Measurement & Data: Classify objects and count the number of objects in each category.

3. Classify objects into given categories; count the numbers of objects in each category and sort the categories by count.

Tip the Scales
Number of People: 1   Time: 15 minutes   Grade Level **K**

Materials: Food scale, various types of food
Description: A food scale is a great source of math activities. Let your child hold an apple in one hand and a peach in the other. Which is heavier? Use the scale to check the weight of both. She'll want to try a variety of items to see how often she's right. A bigger challenge is to see how close she can get to guessing the weight of the apple.

MATH LEARNING STANDARD
Measurement & Data: Describe and compare measurable objectives.
1. Describe measurable attributes of object, such as length or weight. Describe several measurable attributes of a single object.

Store Shapes
Number of People: 1+   Time: Varies   Grade Level **K**

Materials: Grocery Store
Description: Teach your child about different shapes such as cylinders, circles, squares, cubes, spheres, cones, and rectangles. At the grocery store, tell your child to show you all the cylinders he can find. Then, have him find as many squares as possible. There are all kinds of shapes in the store. See how many items your child can find of each shape.

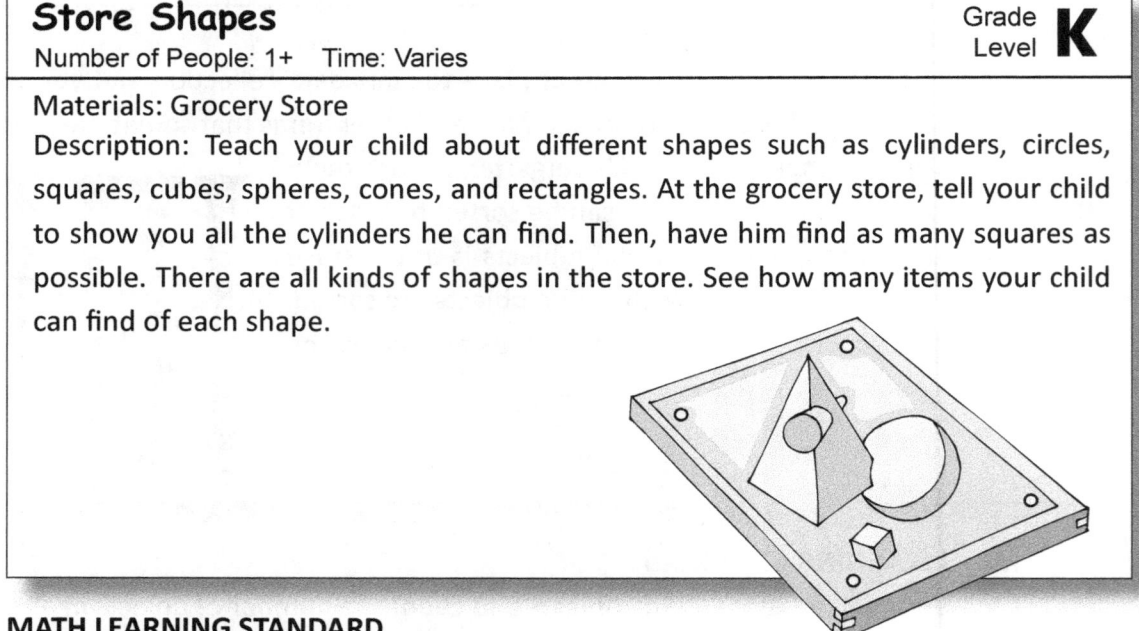

MATH LEARNING STANDARD
Geometry: Identify and describe shapes (squares, circles, triangles, rectangles, hexagons, cubes, cones, cylinders, and spheres).
2. Correctly name shapes regardless of their orientations or overall size.

STARt counting!

Family Math Night at Home

Number of People: Many Time: 2 hours

Grade Level **K**

Materials: Invitation to your schools Family Math Night

Description: School events like Family Math Night are great for helping parents and children enjoy math together. Parents and children get to do fun math activities at various locations around the school. Tangrams and building a marshmallow tower are two examples. Play these games at home with the whole family.

MATH LEARNING STANDARD

Geometry: Analyze, compare, create, and compose shapes

5. Model shapes in the world by building shapes from components and drawing shapes.

What we learned today...

_____

_____

_____

_____

_____

_____

_____

Volume of Groceries

Number of People: 2   Time: A few minutes   Grade Level: K

Materials: Paper bag, grocery items in your cupboard
Description: Fill a lunch bag with miscellaneous items such as an apple, ping pong ball and paper-clip. Have your child pull an item from the bag and describe its size, shape, weight, length, or other attributes. Repeat this until the bag is empty.

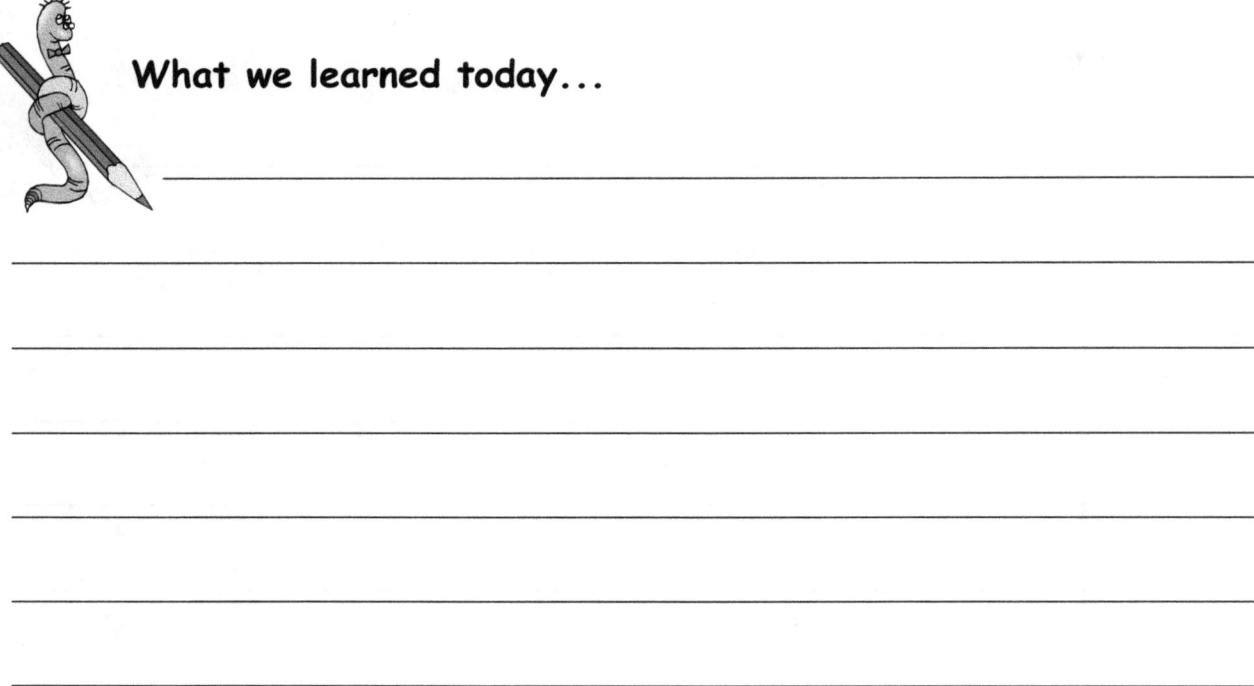

MATH LEARNING STANDARD

Measurement & Data: Describe and compare measurable attributes

1. Describe measurable attributes of objects, such as length or weight. Describe several measurable attributes of a single object.

What we learned today...

_____
_____
_____
_____
_____
_____

Who's Coming to Dinner

Number of People: 2   Time: 10-15 minutes

Grade Level **1**

Materials: Dinnerware

Description: When preparing dinner, there are many ways to do math. Have your child put the silverware out for a family dinner. How many spoons will be needed? Forks? Knives? How many plates? Invite friends for dinner and do it again. What happens when someone in the family isn't home for dinner?

MATH LEARNING STANDARD

Operations & Algebraic Thinking: Represent and solve problems involving addition and subtraction

1. Use addition and subtraction with 20 to solve word problems involving situations of adding to, taking from, putting together, taking apart, and comparing, with unknowns in an all positions.

What we learned today...

_____

_____

_____

_____

_____

_____

Dice Add

Number of People: 2+   Time: 15-30 minutes

Grade Level **1**

Materials: Dice set

Description: There are several ways to play games with dice. Throw a pair of dice and have your child write the numbers down as a math problem. For example, 4+2=___. Have her fill in the blank. Then, it's your turn. Have her check to make sure your answer is correct.

MATH LEARNING STANDARD

Operations & Algebraic Thinking: Work with addition and subtraction equations.
7. Understand the meaning of the equal sign, and determine if equations involving addition and subtraction are true or false.

Christmas Count

Number of People: 2   Time: 15 minutes

Grade Level **1**

Materials: Christmas tree with all its decorations, presents

Description: My kids like to count the Christmas presents under the tree. Have your kids do the same. While they're counting, have them count other things like the red, blue, and green ornaments. How many total ornaments? How many lights are blinking? Have them record their answers. If you celebrate the holiday season in another way, find things to count in your way of celebrating.

MATH LEARNING STANDARD

Number & Operations in Base Ten: Extend the counting sequence
1. Count to 120, starting at any number less than 120. In this range, read and write numerals and represent a number of objects with a numeral

Diamonds look a bit like STARs.

Card Add and Subtract

Number of People: 2   Time: 15 minutes   Grade Level: 1

Materials: A deck of cards without the face cards

Description: Take turns drawing two cards. The other person gets to decide before the draw if the one drawing will add or subtract the two cards drawn. For example, 4 of hearts, plus 2 of spades, or 9 of diamonds, minus 2 of clubs.

MATH LEARNING STANDARD

Operations & Algebraic Thinking: Add and subtract within 20

6. Add and subtract within 20, demonstrating fluency for addition and subtraction within 10.

What we learned today...

_____

_____

_____

_____

_____

_____

Is there a STARfish in that bag?

Grocery Guess
Number of People: 2   Time: 30 muntes

Grade Level **1**

Materials: Bag of groceries, scale
Description: Choose three objects from your grocery bag. Have your child guess which one is longest. Measure the objects with a ruler or tape measure to see if he was right. Which is longest? Which is the shortest?

MATH LEARNING STANDARD

Measurement & Data: measure lengths indirectly and by iterating length units.
1. Order three objects by length; compare the lengths of two objects indirectly by using a third object.

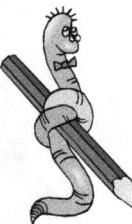

What we learned today...

_____

_____

_____

_____

_____

_____

LEGO® Language

Number of People: 1+ Time: 15 minutes Grade Level **1**

Materials: Set of Legos

Description: Most kids like Legos, and Legos are helpful in teaching about shapes and structure. Let your child create different objects. For example, she can create a tower; take it apart and create a round object; take it apart, and create a spaceship.

MATH LEARNING STANDARD

Geometry: Reason with shapes and their attributes

2. Compose two-dimensional shapes or three-dimensional shapes to create a composite shape, and compose new shapes from the composite shape.

License Plate Math

Number of People: 1+ Time: varies Grade Level **2**

Materials: Car

Description: In the car, we play a license plate game. We look for equations with the numbers on the license plates of nearby vehicles. Add the first two numbers on the plate. For example, 4+5=? As skills improve, add the first three numbers on the plate, 4+5+3=? Change the game and have the first two numbers become one. For example, 453VUG becomes 45. Add 45 to 3. 45+3=___. If you have more than one child in the car, they can take turns or compete for who can add the numbers the fastest.

MATH LEARNING STANDARD

Number & Operations in Base Ten

Fluently add and subtract within 100 using strategies based on place value, properties of operations, and/or the relations between addition and subtractions

Inventory Your Stock
Number of People: 2   Time: 30+ minutes   Grade Level **2**

Materials: Screws in the garage, beans in the kitchen
Description: Have your child help record your inventory, such as screws in the garage or beans in the kitchen. How many do you have? Are there different kinds? It might be easier to sort them into piles of 10 first.

MATH LEARNING STANDARD

Number & Operations in Ten: Understand place value
2. Count within 1000; skip-count by 5s, 10s, and 00s.

Money Cube Game
Number of People: 2   Time: 30 minutes   Grade Level **2**

Materials: Several coins, number cube
Description: Start the game with a pile of coins. Have your child roll a number cube. She gets the number of pennies that comes up on the cube. Then, you take a turn. When she gets five pennies, have her exchange it for one nickel. When she gets 10 cents, have her exchange it for one dime. Have her help you exchange your coins. The first one to get $1 in coins wins.

MATH LEARNING STANDARD

Measurement & Data: Work with time and money
8. Solve word problems involving dollar bills, quarters, dimes, nickels and pennies, using a.m. and p.m., using $ and ¢ symbols appropriately.

If you have trouble, try reSTARting.

Change Game
Number of People: 1   Time: 10-20 minutes

Grade Level **2**

Materials: Coins

Description: Hold several coins in your hand. Say something like, "I have 12 cents and three coins in my hand. What coins do I have?" Your child needs to visualize coins, know their value, and add them up. Repeat this. As a reward, give him the highest amount he gets correct.

MATH LEARNING STANDARD

Measurement & Data: Work with time and money

8. Solve word problems involving dollar bills, quarters, dimes, nickels and pennies, using a.m. and p.m., using $ and ¢ symbols appropriately.

What we learned today...

_____

_____

_____

_____

_____

_____

Laundromat Change

Number of People: 2   Time: 20 Minutes   Grade Level **2**

Materials: Laundry, Laundromat, change

Description: If you visit the Laundromat, take your child with you. Have your child help you gather the correct change and put the change into the machines.

MATH LEARNING STANDARD

Operations and Algebraic Thinking: Represent and solve problems involving addition and subtraction

1. Use addition and subtraction within 100 to solve one– and two-step word problems involving situations of adding to, taking from, putting together, taking apart, and comparing, with unknowns in all positions.

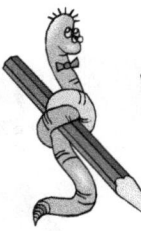 **What we learned today...**

_____

_____

_____

_____

_____

_____

Play Store

Number of People: 2   Time: 30+ minutes

Grade Level **2**

Materials: Food items, stickers, marker

Description: Play store together. Have your child decide the prices of the items. You can pretend to be the customer buying two cans of tomatoes and a carton of eggs. You won't need to use cents/decimals yet. Just have everything cost dollar amounts (e.g., $1 for each can of tomatoes, $2 for a carton eggs, and $5 for ground beef). How much do you owe?

MATH LEARNING STANDARD

Numbers & Operations in Base Ten: Use place value understanding and properties of operations to add and subtract.

7. Add and subtract within 1000, using concrete models or drawings and strategies based on place value, properties of operations, and/or the relationship between addition and subtraction; relate the strategy to a written method.

Gifts and Ribbons

Number of People: 2   Time: An hour or so

Grade Level **2**

Materials: Gift, ribbon, a yard stick

Description: Wrapping packages is always fun. How many yards of ribbon will you need to wrap all your gifts? Let your child estimate the amount, and then measure it for you as you wrap each one. Which gift took the most ribbon? Which took the least? How close was the estimate to the yards of ribbon you actually used?

MATH LEARNING STANDARD

Measurement & Data: Measure and estimate lengths in standard units

3. Estimate lengths using units of inches, feet, centimeters, and meters.

Getting a Feel for Time

Number of People: 1   Time: A week or so   Grade Level **2**

Materials: Chart paper, watch, pencil

Description: My son James tells me he never gets any playtime. When he also said it took him an hour to take out the trash, I decided to teach him about time. Help your child record how long it actually takes to do certain chores. Then do the same for play activities. Help your child make a simple graph to show the time for work and play.

MATH LEARNING STANDARD

Measurement & Data: Represent and interpret data

10. Draw a picture graph and a bar graph to represent a data set with up to four categories. Solve simple put-together, take-apart, and compare problems using information presented in a bar graph.

Bingo Cards

Number of People: 2   Time: 15 minutes   Grade Level **2**

Materials: Paper, pencil and ruler

Description: Kids like to play bingo. Making your own bingo cards is fun and helps promote math skills. Give your child a rectangular piece of paper. (Half of a sheet of copy paper works well.) Help him fold the paper into equal rows and columns. How many squares are there? Now, you'll be ready to fill in the squares with numbers for a bingo game.

MATH LEARNING STANDARD

Geometry: Reason with shapes and their attributes

2. Partition a rectangle into rows and columns of same-size sqares and count to find the total number of them.

I've always been partial to cuSTARd pie!

Pie or Cake?

Number of People: 2 Time: 15 minutes

Grade Level **2**

Materials: Pies or cakes (or pictures of pies or pan cakes)

Description: Have your child cut a piece of cake into two equal pieces. How about three equal pieces? Now, four. Look at them together to decide if the pieces are equal. Then, enjoy the cake.

MATH LEARNING STANDARD

Geometry: Reason with shapes and their attributes

3. Partition circles and rectangles into two, thee, or four equal shares, describe the shares using the words halves, thirds half or, a third of, etc. and describe the whole as two halves, three thirds, four fourth. Recognize that equal shares of identical wholes need not have the same shapes.

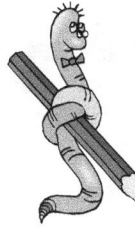

What we learned today...

_____

_____

_____

_____

_____

_____

Page 75

Do you know the state that has a STAR on their license plate?

Collectables
Number of People: 1+   Time: 10-20 minutes

Grade Level **2**

Materials: Jars; a variety of small items

Description: Put a variety of objects into a jar or container—paperclips, bobby pins, screws, bottle caps, keys, etc. Have your child sort the items and mark how many there are of each. How many keys and paperclips? How many more paperclips than keys? You can promote math by using things you'd otherwise throw away. Help your child make a simple graph to show how many are in each.

MATH LEARNING STANDARD

Measurement & Data: Represent and interpret data

10. Draw a picture graph and a bar graph to represent a data set with up to four categories. Solve simple put-together, take-apart, and compare problems using information presented in a bar graph.

Math on Wheels
Number of People: 2   Time: 20 minutes

Grade Level **2**

Materials: Car, license plates, paper and pencil

Description: While traveling, notice a license plate on a nearby car. Using the digits on the plate, see how many 6's there are. For example, if the number is TGY 4631, where are the sixes? The second number is 6. 4+3-1=6. (4+6)-(3+1) = 6. You get the idea.

MATH LEARNING STANDARD

Solve problems involving simple number patterns.

[MA-2.4-2.0-2.2]

What we learned today...

_____

_____

_____

_____

_____

_____

_____

Create your own playbook activities!

Math

Number of People: Time: Grade Level

Materials:

Description:

MATH LEARNING STANDARD

Math

Number of People: Time: Grade Level

Materials:

Description:

MATH LEARNING STANDARD

Create your own playbook activities!

Math

Number of People:　　　　Time:　　　　　　　　　　Grade Level

Materials:

Description:

MATH LEARNING STANDARD

Math

Number of People:　　　　Time:　　　　　　　　　　Grade Level

Materials:

Description:

MATH LEARNING STANDARD

SCIENCE

K – 2

Parent Playbook Activities

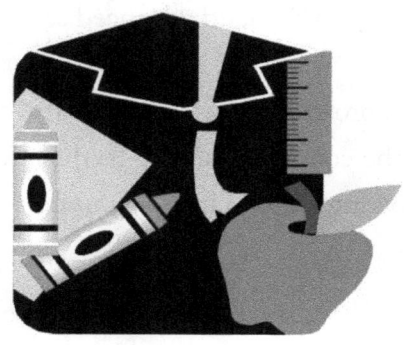

Want to add your favorite activity to the next Parent Playbook?
Use the convenient form in the back of this book or contact the publisher at:

www.familyfriendlyschools.com • www.engagepress.com

By Dr. Joni Samples   **SCIENCE LEARNING STANDARDS**

SCIENCE LEARNING STANDARDS
Grades K-2

The purpose of learning standards is to enable all students to achieve scientific literacy. The standards used for the activities on the following pages are a compilation of standards used in districts across the nation.

The K-8 standards are a continuous roadmap of knowledge building one skill upon another. This roadmap tells us how to get to the final destination. Scientific literacy is of increasing importance in our workplace. More and more jobs demand advanced science skills.

The Science Learning Standards provide expectations for the development of student understanding and ability over the course of their K-8 education. We have listed the Science Learning Standards on the following page to help you understand how each activity connects to each standard.

Standard A: Science as Inquiry
- Abilities necessary to do scientific inquiry
- Understanding about scientific inquiry

Standard B: Physical Science
- Properties of objects and materials
- Position and motion of objects
- Light, heat, electricity, and magnetism

Standard C: Life Science
- Characteristics of organisms
- Life cycles of organisms
- Organisms and environment

Standard D: Earth and Space Science
- Properties of earth materials
- Objects in the sky
- Changes in earth and sky

Standard E: Science and Technology
- Abilities of technological design
- Understandings about science and technology
- Abilities to distinguish between natural objects and objects made by humans

Standard F: Science in Personal and Social Perspectives
- Personal Health
- Characteristics and changes in population
- Types of resources
- Change in the environments
- Science and technology in local challenges

Standard G: History and Nature of Science
- Science as a human endeavor
- Nature of science
- History of science

Bird Feeder

Number of People: 2   Time: 15 minutes

Grade Level: **K**

Materials: Bird feeder, bird seed

Description: A bird feeder outside your window allows you and your child the chance to see all kinds of birds. Put up a feeder and learn about different types of birds. Count the different types and notice which ones like the food the best.

SCIENCE LEARNING STANDARD A 2

Kids learn how to observe and describe similarities and differences in the appearance and behavior of plants and animals.

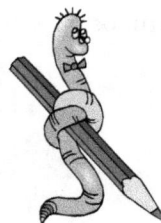

What we learned today...

_____

_____

_____

_____

_____

_____

_____

Science Toys
Number of People: 1+   Time: 15 minutes or so   Grade Level **K**

Materials: Science toys

Description: Ant farms, goldfish, tomato plants, and magnifying glasses can serve as fun science projects. They make great presents that promote lasting learning. What more could you ask for?

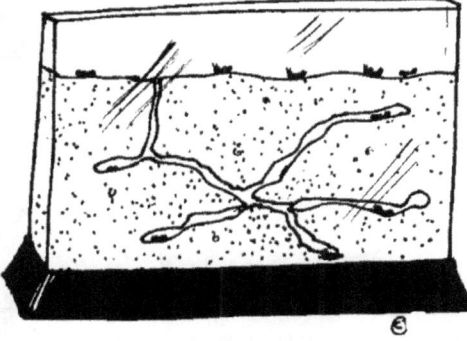

SCIENCE LEARNING STANDARD A 2
Students learn how to observe and describe similarities and differences in the appearance and behavior of plants and animals by asking questions.

Bath Time
Number of People: 1   Time: 20 minutes   Grade Level **K**

Materials: Toys in the bathtub

Description: Kids like playing with toys in the bathtub. Why do some items float? A rock doesn't float. Why does a rubber ducky float? The word is density. A rock has more density than their toy. Let them try several items to check out the density. Find out which ones float. (Just make sure they have their own rubber ducky and not yours).

SCIENCE LEARNING STANDARD B 1
Students learn that objects can be described in terms of the materials they are made of (e.g., clay, cloth, paper) and their physical properties (e.g., color, size, shape, weight, texture, flexibility, attraction to magnets, floating, sinking).

Zoo Visit

Number of People: 2+   Time: Several hours   Grade Level **K**

Materials: Zoo

Description: A visit to the zoo is a real science trip. Where are gorillas? Why are snakes in glass cages? Why do the zebras have stripes? What's the same about the animals? What is different? Take pictures and create a photo album or journal about your trip.

SCIENCE LEARNING STANDARD B 1

Students learn how to observe and describe similarities and differences in the appearance and behavior of plants and animals.

Cubes

Number of People: 2   Time: 20 minutes   Grade Level **K**

Materials: Ice cubes

Description: Why do ice cubes melt? Melt a few and see what happens. Do they melt faster when conditions are warmer? How can you turn the melted water back into an ice cube?

SCIENCE LEARNING STANDARDS B 3

Children learn that water can be a liquid or a solid and can be made to change back and forth from one form to the other by heating and cooling.

Can you guess which kind of matter STARdust is?

Solids, Liquids, Gases
Number of People: 2   Time: 30 minutes

Grade Level **K**

Materials: Various items of matter in different states, e.g. an ice cube, a glass of water, can of soda, cat food, and a pan

Description: Help your child identify the three states of matter—solid, liquid, and gas. Leave an ice cube in a dish while you talk about other things and the cube will change from a solid to a liquid. Discuss other items, such as a glass of water, can of soda, cat food, and frying pan. The glass is solid but the water in it is liquid. The same is true of the can and the soda. The cat food is solid. The pan is solid, the water liquid, but when you heat the water in the pan it becomes steam which is a gas.

SCIENCE LEARNING STANDARD B 3

Students know water can be a liquid or a solid and can be made to change back and forth from one form to the other by heating and cooling.

What we learned today...

_____

_____

_____

_____

_____

_____

When you finish your sandcastle, you might just have a few STARfish move in!

Sand Castles
Number of People: 2   Time: 15 minutes or so

Grade Level **K**

Materials: Sand, water, pails and shovels
Description: Sand castles promote building and designing skills. Children experiment with developing the right mix of sand and water, adding rooms, and tearing down to start again.

SCIENCE LEARNING STANDARD B 3
Students know water can be a liquid or a solid and can be made to change back and forth from one from to the other by heating and cooling.

What we learned today...

_____
_____
_____
_____
_____
_____

Temperature

Number of People: 2   Time: Several months

Grade Level **1**

Materials: Outdoor thermometer

Description: Have your child record the temperature. In the summer, have him track a few days and let you know what part of the day is the warmest. In the winter, what time of day is the coldest? Talk about the differences between seasons.

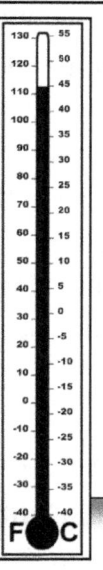

SCIENCE LEARNING STANDARD A 1

Students learn how to use simple tools (e.g., thermometer, wind vane), and skills (observe, measure, cut connect, switch) to measure weather conditions and record changes from day to day and across the seasons.

Environmental Dressing

Number of People: 2   Time: 30 minutes

Grade Level **1**

Materials: A trip through town

Description: As you drive through town, ask your child what kinds of clothes people are wearing. Notice that people tend to dress for the weather. If you live in the desert, you would expect people to dress for heat. If you live in cold climates, you'd expect to see people wearing warm and wooly clothes. Look at the houses and how they reflect the environment—open and airy or steep, pitched roofs. How is the land used? Are there customs that are followed because of the environment, like afternoon naps when it's too hot to work?

SCIENCE LEARNING STANDARD A 1

Students learn that the weather from day to day, but that trends in temperature of rain (or snow) tend to be predictable during a season.

Straw Bubbles
Number of People: 2   Time: 20 minutes   Grade Level **1**

Materials: Straw, a bowl of water with a few drops of liquid soap in it

Description: Kids love to use straws. Have them blow through a straw into a bowl of water with several drops of liquid soap in it. Ask them what's happening. What makes the bubbles? Why do the bubbles go up instead of down? What happens when the bubbles get to the top of the water? Are you dealing with a solid, liquid, or gas? They will either decide they don't like the questions and stop blowing bubbles or they will decide they like science experiments — a winner with either choice.

SCIENCE LEARNING STANDARD B 1

Students learn that solids, liquids, and gases have many observable properties including size, weight, shape, color, temperature. The also have the ability to react to other substances.

Popcorn Science
Number of People: 2   Time: 15 minutes   Grade Level **1**

Materials: Measuring cup, popcorn, oil, pan with lid

Description: Have your child measure 1/4 cup of popcorn kernels. Pop the kernels, and have your child measure what is popped. Why the difference? What happened? What would happen to a 1/2 cup? A whole cup? Enjoy the popcorn with butter and a movie.

SCIENCE LEARNING STANDARD B 1

Materials can exist in different states-solid, liquid, and gas. Properties of substances can change when the substances are mixed, cooled, or heated.

When you shine a light on them, crystals look a lot like STARS!

Crystals

Number of People: 2   Time: A few days

Grade Level **1**

Materials: 3 small glass dishes, warm water, sugar, salt, alum, and a plastic spoon.
Description: Within a short amount of time, you and your child can make your own crystals. Put ½ cup of warm water in each of the three dishes. In the first dish, dissolve as much sugar as you can. Label it "Sugar." In the second dish, dissolve as much salt as possible. Label it "Salt." In the third, put as much alum as the water will hold. Label it "Alum." Put the dishes in a sunny warm place and watch what happens over the next few days. As the water evaporates, crystals will form. What do they look like? Do the three look alike? How are they different? When I was I child, I liked to boil sugar and water together and pour the solution into a tall container. I'd hang strings from the lid of the container and let the crystals form on the string. It's called rock candy and it tastes great.

SCIENCE LEARNING STANDARD B1

Materials can exist in different states-solid, liquid, and gas. Properties of substances can change when the substances are mixed, cooled, or heated.

What we learned today...

_____

_____

_____

_____

_____

_____

I'd reSTARt everyone's coffee after this experiment.

Coffee Leftovers
Number of People: 2 Time: Several Days Grade Level **1**

Materials: Coffee, three cups

Description: Don't throw your old coffee away today. Hand your child three cups of cold coffee, one by one. Put one on the windowsill, one in the refrigerator, and one in a dark cabinet. Leave the coffee to sit for the day. What happens? Are there differences in what happened to each? Why might that be?

SCIENCE LEARNING STANDARD B 1
Students learn that the properties of substances can change when the substances are mixed, cooled, or heated.

What we learned today...

___
___
___
___
___
___

Breakfast Time

Number of People: 2   Time: 15 minutes

Grade Level **1**

Materials: Breakfast cereal and milk

Description: Ask your child what happens to his breakfast cereal when he adds milk to it. What happens to the cereal if you don't eat it for a while? What happens to the milk if you leave it out until lunch? Conduct these scientific experiments as part of your morning routine.

SCIENCE LEARNING STANDARD B 1
Students know the properties of substances can change when the substances are mixed, cooled, or heated.

Crystal Look

Number of People: 1   Time: 20 Minutes

Grade Level **1**

Materials: Magnifying glass, salt, sugar, ice, jar of honey

Description: Let your child go on a crystal hunt with a magnifying glass. Salt, sugar, ice-cube trays, and organic honey in jars are good places to look. Ask about the shape of the crystals. Are they all the same? Where else can you find crystals?

SCIENCE LEARNING STANDARD B 1
Materials can exist in different states: solid, liquid, and gas. Properties of substances can change when the substances are mixed, cooled, or heated.

Plant Care

Number of People: 2   Time: Several weeks

Grade Level: 1

Materials: Planter, soil, seeds, water

Description: Have your child plant a few seeds. As the seeds start sprouting, discuss what happens with one that doesn't get much light or one that got less water than the others. What do plants need in order to grow?

SCIENCE LEARNING STANDARD C 3

Children need direct hands-on experiences with living things, learning about their life cycle and their habitats.

Capillary Action

Number of People: 2   Time: 30 minutes

Grade Level: 1

Materials: Glass of water, red food color, stalk of celery

Description: Kids can learn how water and nutrients travel through a plant. Put a stalk of celery in a glass of water with some red food coloring in it. Have the kids check back every hour or so to see what happens. Discuss what's going on. Why does it change color? What makes that happen?

SCIENCE LEARNING STANDARD D 1

Students learn that roots are associated with the intake of water and soil nutrients and green leaves are associated with making food from sunlight.

If you STARE hard and long enough, you'll find all sorts of fascinating things right before your eyes!

Magnifier Journal

Number of People: 1　　　Time: 20 minutes　　　Grade Level **2**

Materials: Magnifying glass

Description: Give your child a magnifying glass to play detective. Send her on an exploration to find out what's under a leaf, or how many legs a spider has. Are there living things on tree bark? How many different colors can she find in rocks? Have her keep a journal of what she discovers and and engage in daily discussions about her discoveries.

SCIENCE LEARNING STANDARD A 2

Use magnifiers or microscopes to observe and draw descriptions of small objects or small features of objects.

What we learned today...

_____

_____

_____

_____

_____

_____

Centrifugal Force is part of what keeps planets orbiting around a STAR.

Centrifugal Force
Number of People: 2   Time: 5 minutes

Grade Level **2**

Materials: A locket or a bead on the end of a chain

Description: Most kids have tried this out, but they may not know what it's called. Swing a locket, bead, or ball on the end of a string around and around in a circle. If it's going fast enough, the string pulls tight and keeps the end piece going in the circle after you stop swinging. The force that keeps the bead going in its circle is called centrifugal force.

SCIENCE LEARNING STANDARD B 2

Kids learn the way to change how something is moving is by giving it a push or a pull. The size of the change is related to the strength, or the amount of force, of the push or pull.

What we learned today...

_____
_____
_____
_____
_____
_____

Creating a Fulcrum
Number of People: 2   Time: 20 minutes

Grade Level 2

Materials: A small board, a tin can and 3 paperback books

Description: Teach about science with this experiment that involves lifting objects in an interesting way. Have your child place three paperback books on the end of a small board. Lift the board so you can place a tin can on its side under the middle of the board. Have your child press one finger onto the other end of the board to see if he can lift the books. Move the can closer to his finger end of the board and try it again. Now move the can closer to the book end of the board. Try again. What happened with each try? Which was easier? Which method would you use when you need to lift something heavy?

SCIENCE LEARNING STANDARD B 2

Students learn the way to change how something is moving by giving it a push or a pull. The size of the change is related to the strength, or the amount of force, of the push or pull.

Trying Out a Law of Motion
Number of People: 2   Time: 10 Minutes

Grade Level 2

Materials: A swing

Description: Even preschoolers are familiar with Newton's third law of motion. They just don't know the name for it. It states that for every action there is an equal and opposite reaction. There is no motion when you sit still on a swing. But when you push hard against the ground, the swing will move. In which direction does the swing move? After the swing goes far back in reaction to your kick, what happens? You've just experienced Newton's third law.

SCIENCE LEARNING STANDARD B 2

Kids learn the way to change how something is moving by giving it a push or a pull. The size of the change is related to the strength, or the amount of force, of the push or pull.

Magnet Fun

Number of People: 1   Time: 15 minutes   Grade Level **2**

Materials: Magnet

Description: Give your child a magnet and let him see what it will pick up. Will it pick up wood, a chair, or a metal screw?

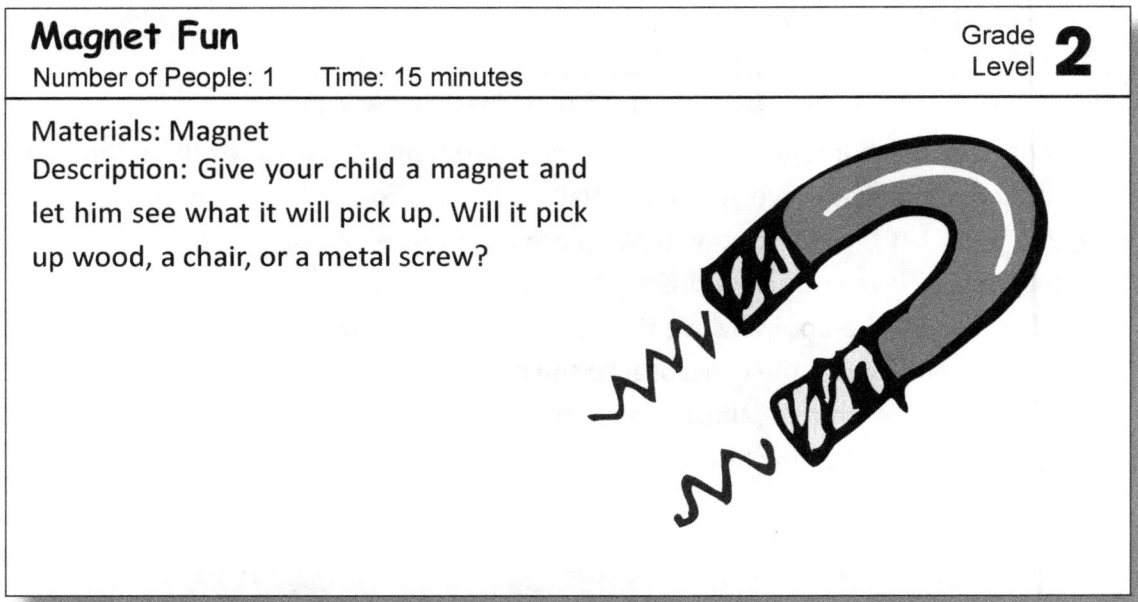

SCIENCE LEARNING STANDARDS B 3

Students learn magnets can be used to make some objects move without being touched.

Wormy Lessons

Number of People: 2   Time: Several weeks   Grade Level **2**

Materials: Plastic shoebox, soil, earthworms

Description: Make a home for earthworms using a plastic shoebox with some soil. Kids love to watch them. Discuss the worms' length, color, and size. When your kids get tired of the worms, you can put them in the garden to help your plants grow.

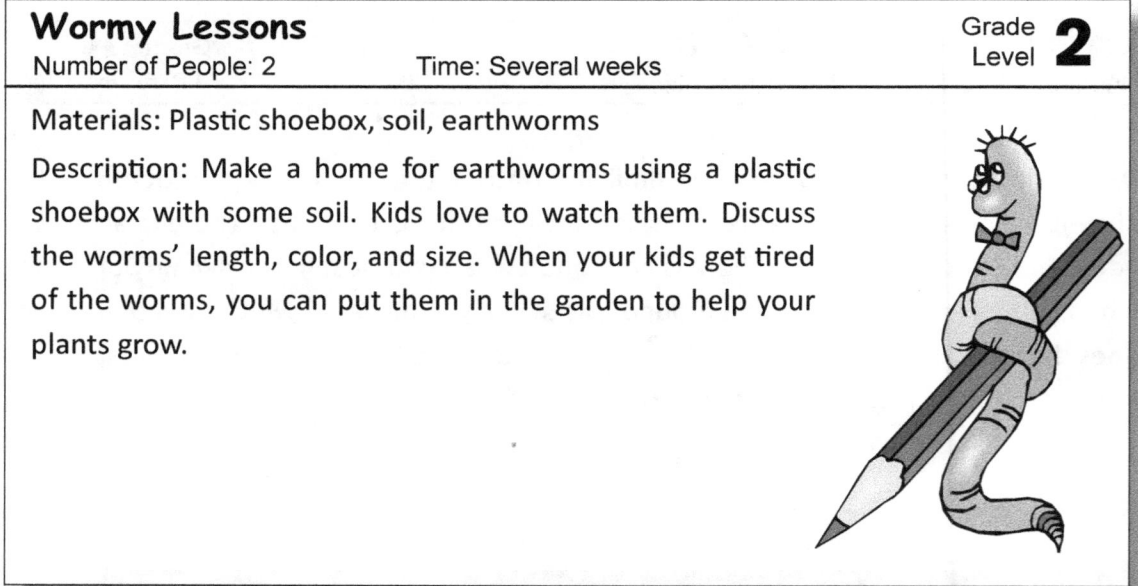

SCIENCE LEARNING STANDARD C 1

Plants and animals have different structure that serve different functions in growth, survival and reproduction.

Flower Time

Number of People: 2   Time: Several days

Grade Level **2**

Materials: Flowering plants and trees

Description: In the spring, ask your child how long it takes a flower to bloom. Does it take longer for some flowers than others? If you have trees in your yard, what happens after the flowers fall? Do you have fruit on your trees? What happens next?

SCIENCE LEARNING STANDARD C 1
Plants and animals have different structure that serve different functions in growth, survival, and reproduction.

What we learned today...

_____
_____
_____
_____
_____
_____

Here's some homework you will be hungry to get STARted on!

Fossil Find
Number of People: 2   Time: 30 minutes

Grade Level **2**

Materials: Brownies with half pecans in them, toothpicks

Description: Kids are often very interested in dinosaurs. Dinosaurs are scary and come in many different shapes and sizes. You can give your children a better understanding of how we discovered dinosaurs. Bake a batch of brownies with nuts (e.g., pecans or walnuts, provided your child isn't allergic to these). Have your child use a couple of toothpicks to see if they can find and extract the nuts. The nuts are like the fossils we find in the rock (brownie). The toothpicks are like the tools archeologists use to find the fossils. Your child will love the search and enjoy eating the results.

SCIENCE LEARNING STANDARD D 1

Students learn that fossils provide evidence about the plants and animals that lived long ago and that scientists learn about the past history of Earth by studying fossils.

What we learned today...

_____

_____

_____

_____

_____

_____

Create your own playbook activities!

Science			Grade Level
Number of People:	Time:		

Materials:

Description:

SCIENCE LEARNING STANDARD

Science			Grade Level
Number of People:	Time:		

Materials:

Description:

SCIENCE LEARNING STANDARD

Create your own playbook activities!

Science
Number of People: Time: Grade Level

Materials:

Description:

SCIENCE LEARNING STANDARD

Science
Number of People: Time: Grade Level

Materials:

Description:

SCIENCE LEARNING STANDARD

HISTORY

K – 2

Parent Playbook Activities

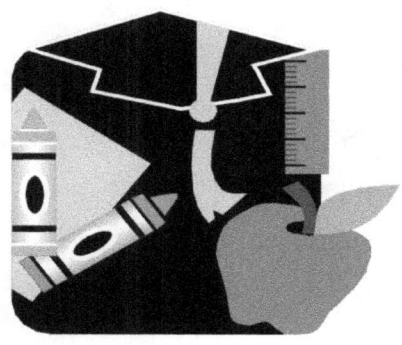

Want to add your favorite activity to the next Parent Playbook?
Use the convenient form in the back of this book or contact the publisher at:

www.familyfriendlyschools.com • www.engagepress.com

By Dr. Joni Samples   History Learning Standards

LEARNING STANDARDS
HISTORY/SOCIAL STUDIES
Grades K-2

The purpose of the History/Social Studies Learning Standards is to enable all students to achieve an understanding of history. The following standards for History/Social Studies are a compilation of standards being used in districts across the nation.

The K-8 standards are a continuous roadmap of knowledge building one skill upon another. This roadmap tells us how to get to the final destination.

The History/Social Studies Learning Standards provide expectations for the development of student understanding and ability over the course of their K-8 education.

We have listed History/Social Studies Learning Standards on the following pages to help you understand how each activity connects to each standard. Also included are the Historical Thinking Standards to help create thoughtful reflection of historic events.

HISTORY
Grades K-2

Standards in history make explicit the goals that all students should have the opportunity to acquire. In history, standards are of two types:

1. Historical thinking skills. Being able to think enables students to evaluate evidence, compare and analyze, be able to explain, and put together sound historical arguments and evaluate and make informed decisions.

2. Historical understandings. This defines what students should know about the history of their nation and of the world. Students learn this through studying the social, political, scientific/technological, economic, and cultural (philosophical/religious/aesthetic) records. These records also provide students the historical perspectives required to analyze contemporary issues and problems confronting citizens today.

Both the World and United States Standards are printed for your information as well as the Historical Thinking Standards.

A NOTE ABOUT THE HISTORY SECTION

The standards in History look very different from other standards listed in this Playbook. Why? Well, the study of history involves much more than the passive absorption of facts, dates, names, and places. History is in essence a process of reasoning based on evidence from the past. This reasoning must be grounded in the careful gathering, weighing and sifting of information such as names, dates, places, ideas, and events. However, the process does not stop here. Real historical understanding requires students to think through cause-and-effect relationships, to reach sound historical interpretations, and to conduct historical inquiries and research leading to the knowledge on which informed decisions in contemporary life can be based.

History itself is a highly integrative field, engaging students in studies not only of the people and of events in their community, state, nation, and world, but opening as well the study of the geographic places in which these events occurred. It includes the ideas, beliefs, and values that influenced how people acted in their daily lives; the rules, laws, and institutions they established and lived by; the oral traditions and the literature, music, art, architecture, and dance they created; and the technological and scientific developments they invented, or adopted, in their quest to improve daily life. In short, studies in history necessarily include geographic, economic, political, social, and scientific studies, as well as studies in the arts.

Historical thinking and understanding do not develop independently of one another. Historical thinking skills enable students to evaluate evidence, develop comparative and causal analyses, interpret the historical record, and construct sound historical arguments and perspectives on which informed decisions in contemporary life can be based. Historical understandings define what students should know about the history of their nation and of the world. These understandings also provide students the historical perspectives required to analyze contemporary issues and problems confronting citizens today.

In the History/Social Studies section of your Parent Playbook the History/Social Studies Learning Standard is listed below the activity. The History/Social Studies Learning Standard and the Thinking Standard are listed by number ... and you may refer back to the beginning of the chapter for the actual standard.

HISTORY LEARNING STANDARDS
Grades K-2

Standards in history make explicit the goals that all students should have the opportunity to acquire. In history, standards are of two types:

1.   Historical thinking skills. Being able to think enables students to evaluate evidence, compare and analyze, be able to explain, and put together sound historical arguments and evaluate and make informed decisions.

2.   Historical understandings. This defines what students should know about the history of their nation and of the world. They learn this through studying the social, political, scientific/technological, economic, and cultural (philosophical/religious/aesthetic) records. They also provide students the historical perspectives required to analyze contemporary issues and problems confronting citizens today.

Both the World and United States Standards are printed for your information as well as the Historical Thinking Standards for your information.

WORLD HISTORY LEARNING STANDARD
Grades K-2

Era 1: The beginning of Human Society
Standard 1: The biological and cultural processes that gave rise to the earliest human communities
Standard 2: The processes that led to the emergence of agricultural societies around the world

Era 2: Early Civilizations and the emergence of Pastoral Peoples (4000-1000 BCE)
Standard 1: The major characteristics of civilization and how civilizations emerged in Mesopotamia, Egypt, and the Indus valley
Standard 2: How agrarian societies spread and new states emerged in the third and second millennia BCE
Standard 3: The political, social, and cultural consequences of population movements and militarization in Eurasia in the second millennium BCE
Standard 4: Major trends in Eurasia and Africa from 4000-1000 BCE

Era 3: Classical Traditions, Major Religions, and Giant Empires (1000 BCE – 300 CE)
Standard 1: Innovation and change from 1000-600 BCE horses, ships, iron, and monotheistic faith
Standard 2: The emergence of Aegean civilization and how interrelations developed among peoples of the eastern Mediterranean and Southwest Asia, 600-200 BCE
Standard 3: How major religions and large-scale empires arose in the Mediterranean basin, China, and India, 500 BCE - 300 CE
Standard 4: The development of early agrarian civilizations in Mesoamerica
Standard 5: Major global trends from 1000 BCE - 300 CE

Era 4: Expanding Zones of Exchange and Encounter (300-1000 CE)
Standard 1: Imperial crises and their aftermath, 300-700 CE
Standard 2: Causes and consequences of the rise of Islamic civilization in the 7th-10th centuries
Standard 3: Major developments in East Asia and Southeast Asia in the era of the Tang dynasty, 600-900 CE
Standard 4: The search for political, social, and cultural redefinition in Europe, 500-1000 CE
Standard 5: The development of agricultural societies and new states in tropical Africa and Oceania
Standard 6: The rise of centers of civilization in Mesoamerica and Andean South America in the first millennium CE
Standard 7: Major global trends from 300-1000 CE

Era 5: Intensified Hemispheric Interactions (1000-1500 CE)
Standard 1: The maturing of an interregional system of communication, trade, and cultural exchange in an era of Chinese economic power and Islamic expansion
Standard 2: The redefining of European society and culture, 1000-1300 CE
Standard 3: The rise of the Mongol empire and its consequences for Eurasian peoples, 1200-1350 CE
Standard 4: The growth of states, towns, and trade in Sub-Saharan Africa between the 11th and 15th centuries
Standard 5: Patterns of crisis and recovery in Afro-Eurasia, 1300-1450 CE
Standard 6: The expansion of states and civilizations in the Americas, 1000-1500 CE
Standard 7: Major global trends from 1000-1500 CE

Era 6: Emergence of First Global Age (1450-1770)
Standard 1: How the transoceanic interlinking of all major regions of the world from 1450-1600 led to global transformations
Standard 2: How European society experienced political, economic, and cultural transformations in an age of global intercommunication, 1450-1750
Standard 3: How large territorial empires dominated much of Eurasia between the 16th and 18th centuries
Standard 4: Economic, political, and cultural interrelations among peoples of Africa, Europe, and the Americas, 1500-1750
Standard 5: Transformations in Asian societies in the era of European expansion
Standard 6: Major global trends from 1450-1770

Era 7: Age of Revolution (1875-1914)
Standard 1: The causes and consequences of political revolution in the 18th and early 19th century
Standard 2: The causes and consequences of the agricultural and industrial revolution (1700-1850)
Standard 3: Transformation of Eurasian societies in an era of global trade and rising European power (1750-1870)
Standard 4: Patterns of nationalism, State-building and social reform in Europe and Americas (1830-1914)
Standard 5: Patterns of global change in the era of Western military and economic domination (1800-1914)
Standard 6: Major global trends from 1750-1914

Era 8: A Half Century of Crisis and Achievement (1900-1945)
Standard 1: The causes and consequences of political revolutions in the late 18th and early 19th centuries
Standard 2: The causes and consequences of the agricultural and industrial revolutions, 1700-1850
Standard 3: The transformation of Eurasian societies in an era of global trade and rising European power, 1750-1870
Standard 4: Patterns of nationalism, state-building, and social reform in Europe and the Americas, 1830-1914
Standard 5: Patterns of global change in the era of Western military and economic domination, 1800-1914
Standard 6: Major global trends from 1750-1914

Era 9: 20th Century Since 1945-Promises and Paradoxes
Standard 1: How post-World War II reconstruction occurred, new international power relations took shape, and colonial empires broke up
Standard 2: The search for community, stability, and peace in and interdependent world
Standard 3: Major global trends since World War II

Era 10: World History across the Eras
Standard 1: Long-term change and recurring patterns in world history

UNITED STATES HISTORY LEARNING STANDARD - Grades K-2

Era 1: Three Worlds Meet (Beginnings to 1620)
Standard 1: Comparative characteristics of societies in the Americas, Western Europe, and Western Africa that increasingly interacted after 1450
Standard 2: How early European exploration and colonization resulted in cultural and ecological interactions among previously unconnected peoples

Era 2: Colonization and Settlement (1585-1763)
Standard 1: Why the Americas attracted Europeans, why they brought enslaved Africans to their colonies, and how Europeans struggled for control of North America and the Caribbean
Standard 2: How political, religious, and social institutions emerged in the English colonies
Standard 3: How the values and institutions of European economic life took root in the colonies, and how slavery reshaped European and African life in the Americas

Era 3: Revolution and the New Nation (1754-1820's)
Standard 1: The causes of the American Revolution, the ideas and interests involved in forging the revolutionary movement, and the reasons for the American victory
Standard 2: The impact of the American Revolution on politics, economy, and society
Standard 3: The institutions and practices of government created during the Revolution and how they were revised between 1787 and 1815 to create the foundation of the American political system based on the U.S. Constitution and the Bill of Rights

Era 4: Expansion and Reform (1801-1861)
Standard 1: United States territorial expansion between 1801 and 1861, and how it affected relations with external powers and Native Americans
Standard 2: How the industrial revolution, increasing immigration, the rapid expansion of slavery, and the westward movement changed the lives of Americans and led toward regional tensions
Standard 3: The extension, restriction, and reorganization of political democracy after 1800
Standard 4: The sources and character of cultural, religious, and social reform movements in the antebellum period

Era 5: Civil War and Reconstruction (1850-1877)
Standard 1: The causes of the Civil War
Standard 2: The course and character of the Civil War and its effects on the American people
Standard 3: How various reconstruction plans succeeded or failed

Era 6: The Development of the Industrial United States (1870-1900)
Standard 1: How the rise of corporations, heavy industry, and mechanized farming transformed the American people
Standard 2: Massive immigration after 1870 and how new social patterns, conflicts, and ideas of national unity developed amid growing cultural diversity
Standard 3: The rise of the American Labor Movement and how political issues reflected social and economic changes
Standard 4: Federal Indian policy and United States foreign policy after the Civil War

Era 7: The Emergence of Modern America (1890-1930)
Standard 1: How Progressives and others addressed problems of industrial capitalism, urbanization, and political corruption
Standard 2: The changing role of the United States in world affairs through World War I
Standard 3: How the United States changed from the end of World War I to the eve of the Great Depression

Era 8: The Great Depression and World War II (1929-1945)
Standard 1: The causes of the Great Depression and how it affected American society
Standard 2: How the New Deal addressed the Great Depression, transformed American federalism, and initiated the welfare state
Standard 3: The causes and course of World War II, the character of the war at home and abroad, and its reshaping of the U.S. role in world affairs

Era 9: Postwar United States (1945 to early 1970s)
Standard 1: the economic boom and social transformation of postwar United States
Standard 2: How the Cold War and conflicts in Korea and Vietnam influenced domestic and international politics
Standard 3: Domestic policies after World War II
Standard 4: The struggle for racial and gender equality and the extension of civil liberties

Era 10: Contemporary United States (1968 to the present)
Standard 1: Recent developments in foreign and domestic politics
Standard 2: Economic, social, and cultural developments in contemporary United States

HISTORICAL THINKING STANDARDS
Grades K-2

STANDARD 1
The student thinks chronologically: Therefore, the student is able to:

A. Distinguish between past, present, and future time.
B. Identify the temporal structure of a historical narrative or story: its beginning, middle, and end (the latter defined as the outcome of a particular beginning).
C. Establish temporal order in constructing their [students'] own historical narratives: working forward from some beginning through its development, to some end or outcome; working backward from some issue, problem, or event to explain its origins and its development over time.
D. Measure and calculate calendar time by days, weeks, months, years, decades, centuries and millennia, from fixed points of the calendar system: BC (before Christ) and AD (Anno Domini, "in the year of our Lord") in the Gregorian calendar and the contemporary secular designation for these same dates, BCE (before the Common Era) and CE (in the Common Era); and compare with the fixed points of other calendar systems such as the Roman (753BC, the founding of the city of Rome) and the Muslim (622 AD, the hegira).
E. Interpret data presented in time lines by designating appropriate equidistant intervals of time and recording events according to the temporal order in which they occurred.
F. Reconstruct patterns of historical succession and duration in which historical developments have unfolded, and apply them to explain historical continuity and change.
G. Compare alternative models for periodization by identifying the organizing principles on which each is based.

STANDARD 2:
The student comprehends a variety of historical sources: Therefore, the student is able to:

A. Identify the author or source of the historical document or narrative.
B. Reconstruct the literal meaning of a historical passage by identifying who was involved, what happened, where it happened, what events led to these developments, and what consequences or outcomes followed.
C. Identify the central question(s) the historical narrative addresses and the purpose, perspective, or point of view from which it has been constructed.
D. Differentiate between historical facts and historical interpretations but acknowledge that the two are related; that the facts the historian reports are selected and reflect therefore the historian's judgment of what is most significant about the past.

E. Read historical narratives imaginatively, taking into account what the narrative reveals of the humanity of the individuals and groups involved – their probable values, outlook, motives, hopes, fears, strengths, and weaknesses.
F. Appreciate historical perspectives – the ability (a) describing the past on its own terms, through the eyes and experiences of those who were there, as revealed through their literature, diaries, letters, debates, arts, artifacts, and the like; (b) considering the historical context in which the event unfolded – the values, outlook, options, and contingencies of that time and place; and (c) avoiding "present-mindedness," judging the past solely in terms of present-day norms and values.
G. Draw upon data in historical maps in order to obtain or clarify information on the geographic setting in which the historical event occurred, its relative and absolute location, the distances and directions involved, the natural and man-made features of the place, and critical relationships in the spatial distributions of those features and the historical event occurring there.
H. Utilize visual and mathematical data presented in graphs, including charts, tables, pie and bar graphs, flow charts, Venn diagrams, and other graphic organizers to clarify, illustrate, or elaborate upon information presented in the historical narrative.
I. Draw upon the visual, literary, and musical sources including: (a) photographs, paintings, cartoons, and architectural drawings; (b) novels, poetry, and plays; and (c) folk, popular, and classical music, to clarify, illustrate, or elaborate upon information presented in the historical narrative.

STANDARD 3:

The student engages in historical analysis and interpretation: therefore, the student is able to:

A. Compare and contrast differing sets of ideas, values, personalities, behaviors, and institutions by identifying likenesses and differences.
B. Consider multiple perspectives of various peoples in the past by demonstrating their differing motives, beliefs, interests, hopes, and fears.
C. Analyze cause-and-effect relationships bearing in mind multiple causation including (a) the importance of the individual in history; (b) the influence of ideas, human interests, and beliefs; and (c) the role of chance, the accidental and the irrational.
D. Draw comparisons across eras and regions in order to define enduring issues as well as large-scale or long-term developments that transcend regional and temporal boundaries.
E. Distinguish between unsupported expressions of opinion and informed hypotheses grounded in historical evidence.
F. Compare competing historical narratives.
G. Challenge arguments of historical inevitability by formulating examples of historical contingency, of how different choices could have led to different consequences.
H. Hold interpretations of history as tentative, subject to changes as new information is uncovered, new voices heard, and new interpretations broached.
I. Evaluate major debates among historians concerning alternative interpretations of the past.
J. Hypothesize the influence of the past, including both the limitations and opportunities made

possible by past decisions.

STANDARD 4:

The student conducts historical research: Therefore, the student is able to:

A. Formulate historical questions from encounters with historical documents, eyewitness accounts, letters, diaries, artifacts, photos, historical sites, art, architecture, and other records from the past.

B. Obtain historical data from a variety of sources, including: library and museum collections, historic sites, historical photos, journals, diaries, eyewitness accounts, newspapers, and the like; documentary films, oral testimony from living witnesses, censuses, tax records, city directories, statistical compilations, and economic indicators.

C. Interrogate historical data by uncovering the social, political, and economic context in which it was created; testing the data source for its credibility, authority, authenticity, internal consistency and completeness; and detecting and evaluating bias, distortion, and propaganda by omission, suppression, or invention of facts.

D. Identify the gaps in the available records and marshal contextual knowledge and perspectives of the time and place in order to elaborate imaginatively upon the evidence, fill in the gaps deductively, and construct a sound historical interpretation.

E. Employ quantitative analysis in order to explore such topics as changes in family size and composition, migration patterns, wealth distribution, and changes in the economy.

F. Support interpretations with historical evidence in order to construct closely reasoned arguments rather than facile opinions.

STANDARD 5:

The student engages in historical issues-analysis and decision making: Therefore, the student is able to:

A. Identify issues and problems in the past and analyze the interests, values, perspectives, and points of view of those involved in the situation.

B. Marshal evidence of antecedent circumstances and current factors contributing to contemporary problems and alternative courses of action.

C. Identify relevant historical antecedents and differentiate from those that are inappropriate and irrelevant to contemporary issues.

D. Evaluate alternative courses of action, keeping in mind the information available at the time, in terms of ethical considerations, the interests of those affected by the decision, and the long- and short-term consequences of each.

E. Formulate a position or course of action on an issue by identifying the nature of the problem, analyzing the underlying factors contributing to the problem, and choosing a plausible solution from a choice of carefully evaluated options.

F. Evaluate the implementation of a decision by analyzing the interests it served; estimating the position, power, and priority of each player involved; assessing the ethical dimensions of the decision; and evaluating its costs and benefits from a variety of perspectives.

Starting School
Number of People: 2   Time: 30 minutes   Grade Level **K**

Materials: School

Description: Starting kindergarten is a very big deal. It may be the first time your child attends school and it's a brand new place. If the school has a kindergarten tea or get together before school starts, be sure to go. Take your child so he can see the room, the playground, and the cafeteria. Have your child meet the teacher. Explore the classroom and school grounds together. He will be there every day so make sure he's as comfortable as possible.

HISTORY/SOCIAL STUDIES LEARNING STANDARD

National History Standard 1

Understands family life now and in the past, and family life in various places long ago.

National Historical Thinking Standard 1A

Historic Stories
Number of People: 2   Time: 10-15 minutes   Grade Level **K**

Materials: Stories of Famous People

Description: Children love stories. Read or tell them stories about people who model courage, honesty and patriotism. There are wonderful tales about our early leaders. George Washington and Abe Lincoln are good examples. Who else can you think of? Share those stories with your children.

NATIONAL COMPILED SCIENCE STANDARD

National History Standard 1

Understands family life now and in the past, ad family life in various places long ago.

National Historical Thinking Standards 2D and 3D

STARt by identifying where you are on your map.

Map It — Grade Level **K**
Number of People: 2   Time: Several days

Materials: Pencil, paper

Description: Your child will most likely have friends at school from different cultures. Ask her to describe where she thinks a friend's family might come from. Then, look up the country on a map and find information about it on the Internet. Even if your child guesses her friend is from Africa and she's from India, think of the fun you'll have learning about different countries.

HISTORY/SOCIAL STUDIES LEARNING STANDARD
National History Standard 1
Understands selected attributes and historical developments of societies in Asia the Americas, Asia, and Europe.
National Historical Thinking Standards 2G

What we learned today...

_____

_____

_____

_____

_____

_____

_____

Did you know that statues are really just history's megaSTARs?

History Find
Number of People: 2   Time: Dinner time

Grade Level **K**

Materials: Dinner table

Description: Take a walk with your child to learn about history. In my neighborhood, we can take a walk in the park where rocks came from volcanoes, Native Americans once lived, and a movie was made. Our downtown has buildings that are over 100 years old, and we can see statues of famous people. Discuss what you see and the history behind it.

HISTORY/SOCIAL STUDIES LEARNING STANDARD

National History Standard 2

Understand the history of the local community and how communities in North America varied long ago.

National Historical Thinking Standards 2F

What we learned today...

_____

_____

_____

_____

_____

Real Rules

Number of People: 2   Time: 10 minutes

Grade Level: **K**

Materials: None needed

Description: Our country is run according to laws and rules for adults and children. Start a reasonable set of rules when your child is young. Taking turns, sharing, and picking up toys are good examples. As with laws for adults, there are reasonable consequences when children break rules.

HISTORY/SOCIAL STUDIES LEARNING STANDARD

National History Standard 4

Understands how democratic values came to be, and how they have been exemplified by people, events, and symbols

National Historical Thinking Standard 5E

What Would It Have Been Like?

Number of People: 2   Time: 15 minutes

Grade Level: **K**

Materials: None needed

Description: On Columbus Day, ask your child: What did Columbus do, how did he do it, where did he go, why did he go, what would have been different if Columbus had stayed home?

HISTORY/SOCIAL STUDIES LEARNING STANDARD

National History Standard 4

Understands the people, events, problems, and ideas that were significant in creating the history of their state.

National Historical Thinking Standards 2D and 2F

Thanksgiving Activities

Number of People: Family   Time: Dinner time   Grade Level: K

Materials: Thanksgiving dinner

Description: As you enjoy Thanksgiving dinner, talk about how the Pilgrims and Native Americans celebrated the first Thanksgiving. How did they live? How did they get water and food? What did their clothes look like? What were the important things they did and what were the rules they lived by? What would their lives be like if they lived today?

HISTORY/SOCIAL STUDIES LEARNING STANDARD
National History Standard 6
Understands the folklore and other cultural contributions from various regions of the United States and how they helped to form a national heritage.
National Historical Thinking Standards 2D and 2E; 3J

Old Time Life

Number of People: 2+   Time: A few hours   Grade Level: 1

Materials: Trip to a museum
Description: A trip to a local museum promotes all kinds of discussion. You can learn about customs, traditions, living conditions, work, food, dress, games, and how lucky you are to live the way you do today.

HISTORY/SOCIAL STUDIES LEARNING STANDARD
National History Standard 1 and 5
Understands family life now and in the past, and family life in various places long ago.
Understands the causes and nature of movements of large groups of people into and within the United States, now and long ago.
National Historical Thinking Standard 3A and 4B

 It's fun to play make believe. Let's get STARted!

What's In Store

Number of People: 2   Time: 30 minutes or so

Grade Level **1**

Materials: Items from your cupboard, Monopoly money, poker chips
Description: Have your child play "store" with some of the foods you have in your cabinet. Monopoly money is great for this. Be sure to include some home made jam or cookies. Then, you can talk about how things used to be when everyone made their own food, ground the flour, and milked cows.

HISTORY/SOCIAL STUDIES LEARNING STANDARD
National History Standard 1
Understands family life now and in the past, and family life in various places long ago.
National Historical Thinking Standard 1C and 3J

What we learned today...

_____

_____

_____

_____

_____

_____

_____

 I think it would be fun to meet the people who work on a STARship.

Workers and Their Jobs
Number of People: 2   Time: Hour+

Grade Level **1**

Materials: A trip around your neighborhood

Description: Take your child with you to various stores and markets in your neighborhood. Take a few extra minutes when you're in each store to talk to people who work there. Ask about what they do, how they get the things they sell, and why they sell them. Have your child save money, from her allowance or by doing chores, so she can purchase one of those items.

HISTORY/SOCIAL STUDIES LEARNING STANDARD
National History Standard 1
Understands family life now and in the past, and family life in various places long ago.
National Historical Thinking Standards 5D, 5E, and 5F

What we learned today...

_____

_____

_____

_____

_____

_____

_____

Environmental Dressing

Number of People: 2   Time: 30 Minutes   Grade Level 1

Materials: A trip through town

Description: As you drive through town, ask your child what kinds of clothes people are wearing. You took this same kind of drive in a science activity in this book when the discussion was about weather. This time look at the environment. Notice that people tend to dress for the environment. If you live in the desert, you would expect people to dress for heat. If you live in cold climates, you'd expect warm and wooly clothes. Look at the houses and how they reflect the environment—open and airy or steep pitched roofs. How is the land used? Are there customs that are followed because of the environment? How has the history of the environment affected the history of the town?

HISTORY/SOCIAL STUDIES LEARNING STANDARD
National History Standards 3
Understands the people, events, problems, and ideas that were significant in creating the history of their state.
National Historical Thinking Standard 3 C

Family History

Number of People: 2   Time: An hour or so   Grade Level 1

Materials: Pictures, paper, glue, yarn

Description: Explore your family's history together. Look through your old pictures. Identify who's in the pictures and when the pictures were taken. Put them in chronological order. Talk about the people in the pictures and what was happening in the community when the pictures were taken. Create a photo album together.

HISTORY/SOCIAL STUDIES LEARNING STANDARD
National History Standard 3
Understands the people, events, problems, and ideas that were significant in creating the history of their state.
National Historical Thinking Standard 1D, 1E, and 1F

Recite the Pledge
Number of People: 2   Time: 30 Minutes

Grade Level **1**

Materials: Copy of the Pledge of Allegiance

Description: Children recite the Pledge of Allegiance every day at school, but they may not know what the words mean. Take a few minutes to go through the words, one at a time, and talk about what they mean:

    I: an individual of one

    pledge: promise

    allegiance: loyalty

and so on. If you need some help, the comedian Red Skelton did a piece on this a number of years ago. If you can find it on the Internet, you and your child might enjoy watching it.

HISTORY/SOCIAL STUDIES LEARNING STANDARD

National History Standard 4

Understands how democratic values came to be, and how they have been exemplified by people, events, and symbols.

National Historical Thinking Standard 4A and 5B

They Are Us
Number of People: 2   Time: Hour+

Grade Level **1**

Materials: A movie with characters from a different culture

Description: After watching a movie, talk about the similarities and differences between the characters. How are the characters different from you in terms of language, clothes, shelter, health, or any other factors ? What are the similarities?

HISTORY/SOCIAL STUDIES LEARNING STANDARD

National History Standard 5

Understands the causes and nature of movements of large groups of people into and within the United State, now and long ago.

National Historical Thinking Standard 3B

Can you name a country that is known for its STARkness?

Continental Surroundings
Number of People: 2   Time: A globe or a world map

Grade Level **1**

Materials: Paper and pencil, research sources – history book, Internet
Description: Name a country. Have your child locate the country on a map or globe. Then have them tell you which continent the country is in. Ask them to name of other countries in the same continent.

HISTORY/SOCIAL STUDIES LEARNING STANDARD
National History Standard 7
Understands selected attributes and historical developments of societies in Africa, the Americas, Asia, and Europe.
National Historical Thinking Standard 2G

What we learned today...

_____

_____

_____

_____

_____

_____

Many inventors were considered the megaSTARs of the 20th and 21st century.

Find It

Number of People: 2   Time: 15 minutes

Grade Level **1**

Materials: World map, United States map

Description: Every mechanical device your child sees started as someone's idea—a cell phone, car, TV, DVD player, computer. They were all invented by someone. Play a game to see who can find out the inventor of an item. When was it invented? How do we enjoy the benefits of that invention? How would life be different without this invention?

HISTORY/SOCIAL STUDIES LEARNING STANDARD
National History Standard 8
Understand major discoveries in science and technology, some of their social and economic effects, and the major scientists and inventors responsible for them.
National Historical Thinking Standard 5B and 5D

What we learned today...

_____
_____
_____
_____
_____
_____
_____

Historical Secrets

Number of People: 2   Time: 30 minutes   Grade Level **2**

Materials: Map of the North American Continent

Description: We used maps a lot in our family. On trips, the kids followed the maps as we traveled. Use maps to identify cities, counties, and states. How far is it from the city you are in to the next stop? Do you pass through any county lines or into another state on the way?

NATIONAL COMPILED \HISTORY/SOCIAL STUDIES STANDARD
National History Standard 2
Understand the folklore and other cultural contributions from various regions of the United States and how they helped to form a national heritage.
National Historical Thinking Standards 2b and 2D

Vacation

Number of People: 2+   Time: Several Hours   Grade Level **2**

Materials: A trip through your State

Description: On your next vacation, you'll pass through a variety of locations. Use the trip as a chance to talk about the areas and how they are the same or different from each other; urban, suburban, and rural. Notice the big cities with the buildings and traffic; drive through residential neighborhoods; take a look at the hills and farms in the rural areas. What were the areas like 10 years ago, 25, 50, or even 100 years ago?

NATIONAL COMPILED \HISTORY/SOCIAL STUDIES STANDARD
National History Standard 2
Understands the history of the local community and how communities in North America varied long ago.
National Historical Thinking Standard 2D and 2E

Sorting Family Pictures and Histories

Number of People: 2 Time: 20 minutes

Grade Level **2**

Materials: Your memory, a history book or the Internet

Description: History is full of famous people. This activity involves pretending to be one of them. You can narrow the field, for example, by picking an era. Early American leaders is a good one. Let your child pretend to be one of them and you guess who they are. George Washington, Benjamin Franklin, Betsy Ross, Benedict Arnold, or Thomas Jefferson are possibilities. Let her pick one and describe things about that leader or things they did until you can guess who they are. Then, you can pretend to be someone famous in the era you've chosen and let them guess who you are.

HISTORY/SOCIAL STUDIES LEARNING STANDARD

National History Standard 2

Understands the history of the local community and how communities in North America varied long ago.

National Historical Thinking Standards 1D, 1E, and 1F

Family Histories

Number of People: 2+ Time: Hour+

Grade Level **2**

Materials: Map

Description: What's your family's ancestry? If you're not sure, talk about this with relatives who may know, or do some internet research together. Look up the locations on a map. How far is that from where you live now? When did they get here, how, and why?

HISTORY/SOCIAL STUDIES LEARNING STANDARD

National History Standards 5

Understand the causes and nature of movements of large groups of people into and within the United States, now and long ago.

National Historical Thinking Standard 3A, 3B, and 3D

I come from a big family of STARgazers, how bout you?

Where Are You From?

Number of People: 2   Time: 30 minutes or so   Grade Level **2**

Materials: Conversations with family members

Description: The population of the United States grew from 40 million people in 1870 to 123 million in 1930. Most of the growth was people from other countries. Find out where your family is from. You may be very clear about being Irish or German, or it may be you don't know much about your background. Help your child create a family tree. Grandparents may be a good source of information. Find out when they were growing up what food they ate, where they got it, and who prepared it. What clothes did they wear? Do we wear those clothes today? Do you still eat some of those foods today? Discuss your findings with the rest of the family.

HISTORY/SOCIAL STUDIES LEARNING STANDARD
National History Standards 6
Understands the folklore and other cultural contributions from various regions of the United States and hw they helped to form a national heritage.
National Historical Thinking Standards 4B, 4C, and 4D.

What we learned today...

_____
_____
_____
_____
_____
_____
_____

Great Names

Number of People: 2   Time: Several months

Grade Level **2**

Materials: Stories and autobiographies of great leaders and heroes
Description: History is full of many great people Help your child find out about people like Lincoln, Louis Pasteur, Sitting Bull, George Washington Carver, Jackie Robinson, Sally Ride, and others. Books and the Internet are good sources of information.

HISTORY/SOCIAL STUDIES LEARNING STANDARD
National History Standards 6
Understand the folklore and other cultural contributions from various regions of the United States and how they helped to form a national heritage.
National Historical Thinking Standard 2A and 2B.

What we learned today...

_____
_____
_____
_____
_____
_____
_____

Farm Visit

Number of People: 2+   Time: An afternoon

Grade Level **2**

Materials: Visit to a farm

Description: On a weekend afternoon, visit a farm. Tell your child he can ask questions, and I bet he will. Most kids are really curious about chickens, cows, corn, and pumpkins. Most farmers are willing to talk about what they do, where and how the crops are distributed, what affect the weather has on their growth and many other questions. Be sure to ask the farmer what technology is used on the farm. Things have changed in the last 50 years.

HISTORY/SOCIAL STUDIES LEARNING STANDARD
National History Standard 8
Understands major discoveries in science and technology, some of their social and economic effects, and the major scientists or inventors responsible for them.
National Historical Thinking Standard 1A

Create your own playbook activities!

History
Number of People: Time: Grade Level

Materials:
Description:

U.S. HISTORY LEARNING STANDARDS

HISTORICAL THINKING STANDARDS

History
Number of People: Time: Grade Level

Materials:
Description:

U.S. HISTORY LEARNING STANDARDS

HISTORICAL THINKING STANDARDS

Create your own playbook activities!

History
Number of People: Time: Grade Level

Materials:

Description:

U.S. HISTORY LEARNING STANDARDS

HISTORICAL THINKING STANDARDS

History
Number of People: Time: Grade Level

Materials:

Description:

U.S. HISTORY LEARNING STANDARDS

HISTORICAL THINKING STANDARDS

INDEX

ENGLISH LANGUAGE ARTS (ELA)

	Page
Story Time	6
Beginning to Read Aloud	6
Rebus Writing	7
Favorite Topics	8
Write Right	9
Double Duty Bookmarks	9
While Reading the Newspaper	10
Alphabet Fun	10
Alphabet Game	11
Keyboard Letters	12
Rhymes	13
Rhyme Time	13
Computer Letters	14
Word Families	14
Learning to Read Comes in Steps	15
Tell Me A Story	16
Stories Out Loud	17
Stories to Tell	17
Alphabet Write	18
Catalog Trails	18
Travel Game	19
Stick It Notes	20
Stories Out Loud 2	21
Who Tells It?	21
Book Club	22
Read Aloud	22
Grocery List	23
Sentence Scramble	24
Word Groups	25
Word Hunt	25
Find the Words	26
Vocab Bingo	26
Breakfast Read	27
Hard Words	28
My Words	29
Sentence Rearranged	29

What Is It?	30
Write Focus	30
Car Games	31
Books on Tape	32
TV Watching	33
Magazine Book	33
Alpha Write	34
Today, Tomorrow, and Yesterday	34
Who Do You Know?	35
Word World	36
Retell 2	37
Make Reading Fun	37
Read Aloud 2	38
Story and Video	38
Wash Day Read Aloud	39
20 WWWWH Questions	40
Noted Fun	41
Read It to Me Again	41
Reading a Magazine	42
Hard Words	43
Missing Letters	43
Reading Buddies	44
Exercise Your Child's Reading	44
My First...	45
Dry it Write	46
Prompt Me	47
Letters to Grandma	47
Writing Letters	48
Look It Up	48
Can't Get to the Bookstore	49
Stories Out Loud-3	50
Schedule It	51
TV Watching 2	51
TV Listening	52
Drawings Book	52
Directions, Directions	53
Following Directions	54

MATH

Telephone Calls	59
Breakfast Math	59

License Number Recognition	60
War	61
Garage Sort	61
Tip the Scales	62
Store Shapes	62
Family Math Night at Home	63
Volume of Groceries	64
Who's Coming to Dinner	65
Dice Add	66
Christmas Count	66
Card Add and Subtract	67
Grocery Guess	68
Lego Language	69
License Plate Math	69
Inventory Your Stock	70
Money Cube Game	70
Change Game	71
Laundromat Change	72
Play Store	73
Gifts and Ribbons	73
Getting a Feel for Time	74
Bingo Cards	74
Pie or Cake	75
Collectibles	76
Math on Wheels	76

SCIENCE 81

Bird Feeder	84
Science Toys	85
Bath Time	85
Zoo Visit	86
Cubes	86
Solids, Liquids, Gases	87
Sand Castles	88
Temperature	89
Environmental Dressing	89
Straw Bubbles	90
Popcorn Science	90
Crystals	91

Coffee Leftovers	92
Breakfast Time	93
Crystal Look	93
Plant Care	94
Capillary Action	94
Magnifier Journal	95
Centrifugal Force	96
Creating a Fulcrum	97
Trying Out a Law of Motion	97
Magnet Fun	98
Wormy Lessons	98
Flower Time	99
Fossil Find	100

HISTORY 103

Starting School	116
Historic Stories	116
Map It	117
History Find	118
Real Rules	119
What Would It Have Been Like?	119
Thanksgiving Activities	120
Old Time Life	120
What's In Store	121
Workers and Their Jobs	122
Environmental Dressing	123
Family History	123
Recite the Pledge	124
They Are Us	124
Continental Surroundings	125
Find It	126
Historical Secrets	127
Vacation	127
Sorting Family Pictures and Histories	128
Family Histories	128
Where Are You From?	129
Great Names	130
Farm Visit	131

Vote For Who?	133
Next Version	134
Historic Letter: Civil War	134
Famous Women	135
High Tech	136
Labor Union Issues	136
What we learned today...	137
Create your own playbook activities	138

Parent Playbooks Order Form

Grade	# of Copies	Per Copy	Total
Pre-Sch	_____	$19.95	_____
K-2	_____	$19.95	_____
3-5	_____	$19.95	_____
6-8	_____	$19.95	_____
Subtotal			_____
Tax			x _____
Total with tax			_____
Postage / Handling $3.00/bk			_____
Total			_____

Name: _____

Address: _____

City: _____ St: ____ Zip: _____

Phone: _____ Fax: _____

Email: _____

Check or money order #: _____

Purchase Order # _____

Mail to:
Engage! Press
2485 Notre Dame Blvd 370-170
Chico, CA 95928

Or by Fax or Email:
Fax: 530-899-8423
www.familyfriendlyschools.com

Parent Playbooks Activities Form

I have a favorite activity to include in an upcoming parent playbook. It's in the area of:

- [ ] English/Language Arts
- [ ] Math
- [ ] Science
- [ ] Social Studies

Grade Level: Preschool   K-2   3-5   6-8   9-12

Your Name: _____

Address: _____

City: _____ St: _____ Zip: _____

Email: _____

School child attends: _____

Location: _____

Mail to:
Engage! Press
2485 Notre Dame Blvd 370-170
Chico, CA 95928

Or by Fax or Email:
Fax: 530-899-8423
www.familyfriendlyschools.com

Create your own playbook activity

Number of People:	Time:	Grade Level

Materials:

Description:

www.ingramcontent.com/pod-product-compliance
Lightning Source LLC
Chambersburg PA
CBHW080513110426
42742CB00017B/3101